THE POETRY GAMES

Oxfordshire

Edited by Lisa Adlam

First published in Great Britain in 2013 by:
YoungWriters
Remus House
Coltsfoot Drive
Peterborough
PE2 9BF
Telephone: 01733 890066
Website: www.youngwriters.co.uk

Book Design by Ashley Janson

SB ISBN 978-1-78203-343-1

Printed and bound in the UK by BookPrintingUK
Website: www.bookprintinguk.com

FOREWORD

Since our inception in 1991, Young Writers has endeavoured to promote poetry and creative writing within schools by running annual nationwide competitions. These competitions are designed to develop and nurture the burgeoning creativity of the next generation, and give them valuable confidence in their own abilities.

For our latest competition The Poetry Games, young writers from across the country were given the challenge to stand up for what they believe in using nothing but the power of the pen. Using poetry as their tool, these aspiring poets were given the opportunity to express their thoughts and feelings on the topics that matter to them through verse.

Whilst skilfully conveying their opinions through poetry, the writers showcased in this collection have simultaneously managed to give poetry a breath of fresh air, brought it to life and made it relevant to them. Using a variety of themes and styles, our featured poets leave a lasting impression of their inner thoughts and feelings, making this anthology a rare insight into the next generation.

Contents

Henry Box School, Witney

Lord Williams's School, Thame

North Oxfordshire Academy, Banbury

Rye St Antony School, Oxford

THE POEMS

Maimuna

I see her, five,
Bouncing out of school,
Chattering with friends
Smiling, laughing.

I see her again, ten,
Hunch-shouldered, silent,
Like the world is to her,
Like the other children too.

I didn't get it at school today.
I felt stupid, angry.
Nobody understands!

They certainly don't – how can they?
How can they condemn my little sister
To a life of being different,
Of not getting it,
Of them not getting her?

How can they justify –
When their bellows could have fanned her brilliant flame –
How can they justify snuffing it?

I see her yesterday,
Twelve now,
Once more rushing carefree
Alongside friends who understand.

I see her today,
Desolate despair,
About to be taken from a jigsaw into which she fits
And be dumped back,
A square peg in a round hole.
How can they do it? How?

Ciera Connelly-Warne (16)
Bartholomew School, Eynsham

The Youth Of Today

The youth of today are misunderstood
Feared by so many people
The youth of today are thought to be violent
Just because they put on a hood
As soon as this garment
Is placed on their head
The elderly cross the road
As soon as this garment is put on by them
People would rather be dead
When I get cold on a dark winter's night
And put on a hoodie to keep warm
Others cross the road filled with fright
Fearing a stabbing or some weird anger storm
This prejudice view held so many
Really has to be stopped
Because when I get cold on a dark winter's night
I don't want people to run away with fright
Of course there are people that use hoods for crime
For stabbing, killing or worse
But this isn't a society where prejudice rules
Where items of clothing are used as tools
For evil, murder or worse
So next time you go out and see a hoodie
Don't run away screaming with fright
Because that person could be your future PM
Your doctor, your teacher or white knight
So when you see a hoodie
Think again
As that person won't be your end.

Milo Hynes (13)
Bartholomew School, Eynsham

Growing Up!

They started out alright,
Staying out of crime
Being good girls that never cried.
They were good at school
And most other things
And stuff like boys made them cringe.
But along came the famous 13th and everything started to change.

They started wearing make-up
And really short skirts
And got into fights that really weren't worth the
Exclusion from school
And a week's probation
But this seemed to them like it needed a celebration.

The mothers started talking about what to do
As the girls walked out into the gloom,
Knifes in their pockets just in case
Some slutty girl was on their case.
Sometimes they threatened to really use them
But one tough girl could see right through them.

She walked up to them head held high
And everyone thought that she would decline
A fight with the pro in the dark, but she said yes
And heard the gasps. There they stood fists clenched,
Wondering what to do next, one girl stepped forward
And pulled out the knife – the one which killed,
Michaela Bright.

Millie Beaver (14)
Bartholomew School, Eynsham

Crossrail

Slithering down the line
Nearly at the end
All the way from east London
Over to the west
Nearly the last station
Need to do my best.

What a project it was
And what a success it'll be
Although it's only just opened
It's already packed
It's a very popular railway
And that is just a fact!

There is light ahead of us
Further down the line
Applying the brakes
Slowing down
Coming to a halt
In beautiful London town.

The joy – making results of the project
A railway from the east to west
A happy ending for the managers
Because they promised to do their best!

Christopher Loder (11)
Bartholomew School, Eynsham

A Burning Blood

It looked upon me with an unmoving muscle,
Just completely curious . . .

Black as a thousand night skies,
Deep, piercing red eyes stare into your very soul,
Her sharp and vicious fangs shine in the moonlight,
The sable cape flows freely in the cold night air,
Flying ferociously around the glimmering moon,
A puddle of blood around me.

Imaan Razaq (12)
Bartholomew School, Eynsham

My Special Space

When day is ready for its goodbyes
I climb to bed as daylight dies,
As the sun switches with the moon
So sun can rest in her cocoon.

The moon watches, awaiting my glance,
The wind breathes and the curtains dance.
The patterned curtains wave apart,
I look at the moon with love in my heart.

Mother moon hangs bright as day,
Swiftly, gently, sailing away.
I smile at her, she smiles at me,
I am safe, she is free.

I cast a glance at the stars
Bottled up in sphere-like jars.
They twinkle and wink looking for me,
I marvel and look at all I can see.

I snuggle deep in my so special place
So near yet so far from mysterious space.
I smile to myself, it's good to be me,
I close my eyes; this is the place to be.

Annie Lloyd (12)
Bartholomew School, Eynsham

Our Natural World

The bright, beautiful, bluebells bloom brightly in the striking sunny season,
Wonderful waterfalls wind wildly down the wet woodland,
Turning and twisting to take its last breath.
Dark, damp, deep underground caves contain the creepy crawly creatures,
Elks elegantly elongate across the fresh everlasting field,
Snakes slither through the slimy sludge of a mess!
Rapid rain runs down the windows, making me feel as wet as a white whale.
Our wonderful natural world, strikes people like a flash of lightning!

Hannah Tester (11)
Bartholomew School, Eynsham

We Bought A Zoo

My dad came home one day
And said he had bought a zoo!
I screamed and ran upstairs
For he had bought a zoo.
I started packing up my bags
Because we had bought a zoo.
I imagined sparkling animals
Because we had bought a zoo.
I jumped into the car straight away
Because we had bought a zoo.
I smiled at my dad as he came to the car
Because we had bought a zoo.
'What are you doing in there?' he said.
Because we had bought a zoo.
'Help me tend the roses'
Because we had bought a zoo.
'Come on grab a shovel!'
Because we had bought a zoo.
'It does not smell that much!"
Great.
He had bought some poo!

Hannah Elphick (12)
Bartholomew School, Eynsham

Don't Diss Oldies Fam, We Still Love Will.I.Am

If you hate it like I hate it
And you're over sixty-five,
If you want it like I want it
And you feel you're still alive.

If you feel young and beautiful
Then the years will fall away.
Don't wear clothes that are suitable
And moisturise every day.

Can you speak the lingo,
Down at the bingo?
Can you do the limbo,
With your arms akimbo?

Can you feel the love?
Can you feel the love?
Can you feel the love?
Yeah, give old age the shove.

Callum Chapman (13)
Bartholomew School, Eynsham

Baking

I love to make, bake a cake
Pour in all the ingredients and mix them all together!
You could treasure
That moment forever.

I love to make, bake a cake,
Read the recipe book
Then put the cake in to cook.

I love to make, bake a cake,
When the cake is done
Ask your friends to come
All enjoy the cake
I love to make, bake a cake.

Isobel Rees (12)
Bartholomew School, Eynsham

Cuba

An amazing country
With mangoes which are exploding with taste
With the palm trees swaying in the sun.
The parties go on, day and night
Where there's champagne and all.
The beach, fantastic with beach balls, ice cream and bikinis
Or relax at the beach the tide swishing back and forth.
In the day, the sky is like the clearest sea
Amazing blue with the sun which would give you a tan any day.
At sunset, before night, the sky was like light purple crystals
In the sky with a hint of sapphire.
And, when you close your eyes,
You feel the wind blowing in your hair and your mind full of things.

Keisy Lin Fong (11)
Bartholomew School, Eynsham

The City Of Woodlice

A city – under layers of leaves,
Or hidden, in the rotting eaves;
Dripping ceilings and damp floors
Carved by vicious teeth and claws.
Strange creatures roam the corridors –
Cramming wood into hungry jaws,
Forged by weeks of toil and work –
Now, within these walls they lurk.
A city – hidden from our eyes,
The strangest land below Earth's skies;
A labyrinth beneath your floor,
Or in driftwood, on the shore,
It's the city of the woodlice;
Hidden even from nosey mice,
Armoured in rock hard plates,
Dull grey hue, like roofing slates.
A city – under layers of leaves,
Or hidden, in the rotting eaves.

Pedr Davies (13)
Bartholomew School, Eynsham

Hunter

The silence was deafening in the eardrums of the hunter.
The snow crumbled away from his fingers and fell next to the tracks.
With a stone gaze he stared at the stag.
The majestic elegance of its stride left the hunter helpless with admiration.
He stalked it calmly, his brutal axe gently thudding at his side.
His knife glinted in the sharp moonlight.
He drew out his bow, smooth as glass, made of exquisite oak wood.
His last arrow was sleek with a thin shard of flint, shaped like a willow leaf.
For a second his eyes sparked in the moonlight,
The air filled with determination.
The arrow flew in the air and struck the stag's flank.
It fell to its knees.
The last of its magnificence burned out like a flame.
The hunter roared in triumph.

Finn Arbuckle (11)
Bartholomew School, Eynsham

My Favourite Sport

My favourite sport is cricket,
You start by hammering in the wicket.
There are many positions you can play,
Some matches can last all day!

To play cricket you need a bat,
And it might be useful to wear a hat.
Cricket spikes would be good to wear,
As they stop you slipping if the weather is bare.

If you're really good you might hit a four,
Then all of your runs would be put on the door.
If the fielder catches you, they'll shout, 'How's that!'
Then you'll walk off the field with your bat.

Some bowlers bowl with a spin,
They get the batters out so that they don't win.
Normally you will bowl a wicket,
Now that's how you play cricket!

Megan Lovick (13)
Bartholomew School, Eynsham

Writing This Poem!

I sit at my desk
Thinking and wondering
About this marvel of rhymes.

My brain is bustling
My hands are tingling
Of this urge to write and rhyme.

This is a tricky riddle is it not?
This is a puzzling puzzle is it not?
Of all the answers in the world there is still only one.

No one is ever sure of the answer
But people always seem to think that they are
And that has just planted a question in my head!

What is the answer to this poem?

Toby Riley-Cirel (11)
Bartholomew School, Eynsham

Music

When I listen to music
My heart becomes warm
All of my bad emotions
Disappear behind the dawn.

I remember those who are important
And those who I've lost
The lyrics mean the world to me
At any other cost.

The artists are inspirations to me
I listen closely to them
The beat makes me happy
They have my heart condemned.

Every note makes me smile
To see me smile, my mum is happy
Does anyone at all love Dappy
As much as I do?

Toni Purcell (13)
Bartholomew School, Eynsham

Animal Cruelty

Little dogs in tiny bags
Tying hamsters up in rags
Locking cats indoors all day
Not letting rabbits out to play

Leaving pups in cardboard boxes
Leaving chickens out for foxes
Keeping fish in tiny bowls
Poisoning your garden moles

Feeding budgies scraps of meat
Giving snakes nothing to eat
If you see this don't delay
Call the RSPCA!

Sophie Marley (11)
Bartholomew School, Eynsham

A Sonnet To Politics

Shall I compare thee to a banker's bonus
Or a KFC's boneless banquet?
Tax dodgers aren't you anxious?
Considering your targets are so aimless.

Your boondoggle of the financial situation
And enjoy breakfast with sausage and bacon.
You take our parks, our money, so fail to impress,
The poor, the homeless and the NHS.

I bet it's a struggle for your pea-sized minds
As the stocks never make an incline.
So while you have fun and continue to dine
We all struggle and have to fall in line.

And while you laugh and tell us lies
Whatever you do we'll always despise.
So our moods will never brighten
Because your promises will never happen.

Ryan Lanksford (13)
Bartholomew School, Eynsham

Writers' Block

Oh, what to write on my page
I don't know what to do
A poem maybe or story
Someone please help will you

My page is still blank
My pen full of ink
And my brain is dry of ideas
Someone please help me think

A bright spark
An idea at last
Has hit me with greatest force
Now my block has passed

My page is full
My pen is dry
And my brain is stuffed with ideas
My poem is done, adieu.

Holly Butler (12)
Bartholomew School, Eynsham

The Writer Of This Poem

The writer of this poem
Is not at all fat
He is as cool as a koala
When it comes to food he's as keen as a cat

He's as happy as a national lottery winner
He's as fast as a shooting star
As tired as Sleeping Beauty
This writer has not travelled afar

He's as helpful as 999
As smiley as the Cheshire Cat
He's as fun as can be
His favourite word in French is chat

Well it would appear he's ran out of words
The writer of this poem is not at all fat
But if you want to see if the rest is true
You'll have to find out, don't be a lazy cat.

Jack Woodford (12)
Bartholomew School, Eynsham

Man

Frothy, white, wild waves lap at the rocks in silence,
As blue, salty hands caress the soft sand.
Gargantuan, green leaves drift delicately in the faint breeze,
Flowing vines drape against dense, dark trunks.
The peaks of an icecap continue to trickle, but they hold,
As snow does what snow does best, fall.
The world was tranquil . . .
Then Man came.
A black, bleak, bold liquid seeped into the once idyllic ocean,
Putting the remaining wildlife into extinction.
Where proud trees once stood now stand short, sorrowful stumps,
Leaving monkeys, chimps and lemurs to starve.
Blocks of ice break away, slapping the water's surface,
Creating a cacophony of sounds.
This is what Man does to the world,
And what Man does to the world, he ultimately does to himself.

Gina Moran (11)
Bartholomew School, Eynsham

The Elderly

They make you smile, they make you laugh, they make you sad
Getting ready to say hello to your loved ones.
'Hello, lovely to see you, haven't you grown?' they say
They say that all the time you think
But when they go you can't imagine what it would be like without them
So you just laugh and smile

Off food in the fridge, it makes you sad that they don't realise
'It's OK,' they say, 'I'll survive I have until now haven't I?'

Constantly taking about old times
Showing things from back in the day
Stuck in the past you could say.

Getting ready to say goodbye to your loved ones
The memories will never fade
I hope you will remember me
They make you smile, they make you laugh, they make you sad.

Millie Cook (13)
Gillotts School, Henley-on-Thames

Smoking

Smoking is so bad for you,
Why would you want to smoke?
Smoking is so bad for you,
It can cause your death.
Smoke! Smoke! Smoke!

Smoking is so bad for you,
It can damage your heart.
Smoking is so bad for you,
It can ruin your life.
Smoke! Smoke! Smoke!

Smoking is so bad for you,
It's such an addictive thing.
Smoking is so bad for you,
It will make you ill.
Smoke! Smoke! Smoke!

Smoking is so bad for you,
It costs a lot of money.
Smoking is so bad for you,
It can give you cancer.
Smoke! Smoke! Smoke!

Smoking is so bad for you,
It will make you stink.
Smoking is so bad for you,
It will harm your lungs.
Smoke! Smoke! Smoke!

Smoking is so bad for you,
What happens when you kiss?
Smoking is so bad for you,
It makes your skin look old.
Smoke! Smoke! Smoke!

Smoking is so bad for you,
It really isn't cool.
Smoking is so bad for you,
You could have a stroke.
Smoke! Smoke! Smoke!

Smoking is so bad for you,
Have you got the message?
Smoking is so bad for you,
So put your death away.
No smoke! No smoke! No smoke!

Abi Webb (11)
Gillotts School, Henley-on-Thames

The Eat Beat Feast

If you look in the fridge
This is what you will find.
A certain question will come to mind.
Oh what shall I eat, what shall I eat?

A piece of chocolate
Or a piece of cake?
A piece of cheese
Or a drink from the lake?
Oh what shall I eat, what shall I eat?

Too much unhealthy eating will make you fat.
You will have to take a diet.
Blubbery flubbery full of that,
You're too big; you will break a thick wire.

Some grapes or an apple
Will take your fancy.
Some or operation
From your doctor Nancy!

No sweets!
No treats!
No lollipops
We never said that just don't eat a lot.

Walking down the street
Down to the grocery
Finding a few vegetables to eat
You won't hear the question scream and shout
No unhealthy eating, no question coming to mind
Oh what shall I eat, what shall I eat?

Olivia Hope (12)
Gillotts School, Henley-on-Thames

The Call Of Home

As the father left
He waved goodbye.
Dressed up to go
And gave a small sigh.

He checked in the office
And jumped on a plane.
His family afraid
Of not seeing him again.

He got given a gun
And started at war.
His family waiting
Until he knocked on the door.

By the trenches
He holds his breath.
Waiting, waiting
For his death.

Now he lies
In the grass
Hoping for
The war to pass.

The poppies
Magenta red.
The colour of
The blood once shed.

Remind us of
The men who gave
Their lives, their countries
For to save.

Are we the ones who gained from war?
Have we learned from them?
War no more.

Gemma Sarney (12)
Gillotts School, Henley-on-Thames

A Shot Of A Gun

A shot of a gun
The blow of a bomb
The galloping of horses
With more to come.

The hounding of men
Falling to their death
The cries of men
Begging to rest.
Boom! There's a cannon
Bang! There goes a gun
A piercing cry of a mother
Who's just lost a son.

The horses charge forward
Leaving trails of fallen men
Who are soon to stop breathing
Soon to be dead.

Year after year
It's always the same
With men falling to their death
Wishing they'd never came.

And as the last shot fires
With only a percentage still standing
They breathe sighs of relief
And the survivors start clapping but a field still lies
Carrying the dead
And poppies begin to grow
Creating a flowerbed.

And hundreds of years later with our poppies on
Feeling all very solemn
We think is war really the only way
To solve our country's problems?

Jesse Staines (13)
Gillotts School, Henley-on-Thames

A Soldier's Life

He spent months behind enemy lines
His squadron dead, alone,
But now he faces a new battlefield
The one at home.

He straps a pistol to his leg
Carries it wherever he goes
Staying ready, alert,
Hoping nobody knows.

Paranoia takes hold
PTS sets in
He walks alone in the street
Grimacing at the din.

When he drops his kid at school
A father taps him on the shoulder
He grabs him, flips him, puts him on the floor
For you see, you don't touch a soldier.

At lunch he hesitates
The soup on his spoon
For many a night he'd been rationing himself
Under the cold light of the moon.

He hears a bang, the pop of a bag
He lies down instantly, dragging people to the floor
'Get down, get down!' he cries
For he knows nothing more.

He wakes up at 2am, his time to look out
He realises he's home and then falls asleep
He'll have nightmares, the guilt of his actions settling in
And then he'll weep and weep.

This is a soldier's life you see
The one that I chose to adopt for me.

Josh James (12)
Gillotts School, Henley-on-Thames

Poaching Animals

We hate poachers
We love animals
We adore leopards
We love elephants
Let them live.

We love their fur
We love your coats
But not with leopard's skin or fur
I'd rather see them alive up a tree
So let them live.

We love their tusks
We love your carvings and your necklaces
But not with elephant's tusks
I'd rather seen an elephant holding onto its mate than dead
So let them live.

We love tigers
We love your rugs
But not with tiger's fur
I'd rather see one hunt down a muntjac than dead
So let them live.

We love rhinos
We like to be healthy
But not medicine made out of rhino horns
I'd rather see one charging with anger than dead
So let them live.

Please let them live
They are important to the world
It hurts them
And there are not very many left at all
So please let them live!

Jojo Kuspisz (12)
Gillotts School, Henley-on-Thames

Emotions

Love, love is the colour of red like two hearts beating.
The smell of love is sweet like lavender drops.
Love tastes like a sweet chocolate bar, you just want more.
Love feels light and airy like you can jump from cloud to cloud.
Love looks like candyfloss sweet and sticky.

Hate is the colour of darkness.
Hate is the smell of rotten fish.
Hate tastes like sour lemon.
Hate feels like getting thrown out of a house.
Hate looks like a dark cloud of water.

Happy is the colour of pink like a pink rose.
Happy is the smell of sweet peas.
Happy is the taste of ice cream sweet and creamy.
Happy feels like jumping off a jump on your pony.
Happy looks like a wild flower meadow on a sunny day.

Sad is the colour of a light grey.
Sad is the smell of a damp, mouldy, neglected house.
Sad is the taste of stale cabbage.
Sad feels like falling into a muddy puddle.
Sad looks like a misty dull morning across the meadows.

Regret is the colour of dark blue.
Regret is the smell of mouldy cheese.
Regret is the taste of sour milk.
Regret feels like you're in a sinking boat.
Regret looks like water going down a plughole.

Hope is the colour of light red.
Hope is the smell of a lavender candle.
Hope is the taste of fresh air.
Hope feels like fresh clean sheets.
Hope looks like a rainbow.

Maddie McTeague (11)
Gillotts School, Henley-on-Thames

Ninjas

The night air is quiet and smells of dead leaves,
I wander through the trees I have no light.
It is dark out here I walk with quivering knees
For this is the hour with ninjas in sight.

Crack! I hear something behind the big tree.
Snap! It happens again but closer to my ear.
'Help!' I hear someone call out to me.
I have to get ready for the ninjas are near.

I get out my knife hidden in my sleeve,
Then spin around and wait to see one.
A glint in the darkness tells me to leave
But I stay put and wait for the ninjas to be gone.

But then the first one comes without a sound,
I spin to see his knife in my face.
I block it with ease but slowly turn around
To see a ninja behind me holding a mace.

I grab it and throw it away but he kicks me in the gut.
I stumble down to the ground.
He steps on my stomach and raises a weird nut
Then the ninja hits me with it but I hear no sound.

My eyes start going blurry but I stay alive,
I try and get up but stay down.
I look at him and he seems to say, 'Five.'
Five? What does the ninja mean? All I know is that I will die here in my night gown.

Five hits is what he gave me
With his hard hand on my cheek.
Blood comes out my mouth quickly
Then the ninja walks off . . . till next week.

Adam Cookson (11)
Gillotts School, Henley-on-Thames

Stereotyping

Violent, rich, poor, criminal, slut, gay.
That's what they all think and they all say.
Teenagers are violent, aggressive, riot
All they want to do is get drunk and high
That's all they do to make the time go by.
Time is ticking, ticking fast and all the adults look at the past.
The lying papers, the cruel rumours
Apparently we're trying to get our own way.

But that's just what they think and what they all say.

We all like pink, that's what they think.
We like a few drinks, that's what they think.
We're bent, they meant what they said.
All these words flying through my head.
We speak funny with a feminine voice
We're drama queens, we're strange.
Just because we aren't the same.
But who is to blame? Is it us or them?
We're the ones with the problem, just because we're gay.

But that's what they all think and what they all say.

They call me a slut, a slag, a skank; they think I like to go out with whoever.
They think I will never ever endeavour. But no one thought.
They just assume that I'm just the same.
But actually I'm not to blame.
I'm none of those names, it was not my fault
That when someone saw me they came to a halt.
They raped me, raped my dignity, loyalty and trust.
It was not love, only lust.

But that's just what they think and all say

We're no different; we're all the same.

Izzie Larter (13)
Gillotts School, Henley-on-Thames

War And Anthem

What do you think of war?
Boot camp, we don't know but we've been told
Like the ranks, Private, Corporal, Lieutenant, Sergeant Major and General.
We don't know about the consequences like victory.
How many men do we lose?
What about failure? How much do we lose then?
How much land do we need?

What do you see around you?
I see my friends fall beside me
Why did we do this?
I know, because we wanted to be heroes.

Where are we now?
Me and my squad are in enemy lines
We have Tangos down, left, right, centre
We need to get to the extraction point.

Why is there war?
In case there are terrorists and because we are greedy?
If we win we don't get much
If we lose we lose our lives.

What happened to me you ask?
I have been through hell and back
I have heard bullets, gunfire, explosives,
There are buildings falling down.

We thought our plan would work
This is the plan we need to save all the civilians
But the plan went wrong and we got shot at.

Wait, we did it, yes, our plan worked
We could have died but we did not.

Matthew Laye (13)
Gillotts School, Henley-on-Thames

Another Day

Another day of torture
Another day of pain.
Hiding from the bullies,
What are they trying to gain?

Lying in my bed
Very late at night,
Thinking through my head
About yesterday's last fight.

Should I tell my mum and dad,
Would they understand?
I don't know if they'd care
And would they hold my hand?

I'm just sat in the classroom
Then, 'Oh no, here they come!'
With a smirk all over their faces
Is this their idea of fun?

'What do you think you're doing?' they say.
'You don't belong here,' he sniggers.
'Go somewhere else
Or we'll hurt you bigger!'

No friends anymore
They're since long gone.
No, teachers' listen to me
Well, I guess I'm just alone.

This is it
I can't take anymore
So I step out into the road
And lay out on the floor.

Ella Saunders (12)
Gillotts School, Henley-on-Thames

War

Bang!
The bullet whizzed past my head
I woke with a start and got to my feet
The troops had gone
I was all on my own
I wish I was back at home.

Bang!
Another bullet came again and knocked me off my feet
Not a soldier in sight
Not a person to talk to
I got to my feet and brushed myself down.

I was unsure where to go so I walked
Along the sandy embankment and thought to myself

War is an awful thing!
People can die
Grief-stricken families left alone
All to remember, a stone in the ground.

War!
Such blood and deceit
Turning Man against Man
Fighting as an individual group not a world

War
What is the result?
Peace?
Love?
Happiness?
No
War!

Jamie Legg (12)
Gillotts School, Henley-on-Thames

Out Of Sight

I can't sleep
The pressure is building up
The noise is getting deep
I think to myself, *should I have a peep?*

I hear a gunshot
I wonder what it could be
I wonder if they are coming for me

I walk to find
Something to hide behind
When I see
A tall dark shadow
In the meadow
Near a tree

I stand very still
As he moves in for the kill
I slowly turn around
Making no sound
He's seen me
I begin to run
Towards the setting sun

As fast as I can
Away from this terrible man
At last I rest
Out of breath
With the coming of the night
I am finally out of sight.

Sarah White (12)
Gillotts School, Henley-on-Thames

Desperate Hours

Memories of that one last shout
The whole world full of doubt.
Only a few will ever remember
That some families still hurt this December.

Bang, that last sound.
Thud, they're on the ground.
All those soldiers going down.

Eyes black as cold as ice
Like their lives depend on the roll of a dice.
Nothing will ever be the same
All over a pointless, never-ending game.

Bang, that last sound.
Thud, they're on the ground.
All those soldiers going down.

Their hearts beating as loud as drums
Listening to the rumble of death-sending guns.
The world draped in devastation
Hatred spreading through the nation.

Bang, that last sound.
Thud, they're on the ground.
All those soldiers going down.

Peace declared, a future ahead
Time to remember the injured and dead.
Now blood red poppies rise from the ground
At last the world can sleep safe and sound.

Katie Butler (14)
Gillotts School, Henley-on-Thames

The Peace Song

My dad always liked poems,
'The flow of words running smoothly from the tongue,' he said.
But the simple pleasures he often lied, are gone,
And in their place is War – bloody and red.

War is cruel and ruthless,
It seeps into your mind like an endless wailing siren.
It left him in a broken mess,
It left my mother distraught and crying.

Through his eyes I see the streets of war,
Littered with the neglected hopes and worn-out desires.
The children drift alone and afraid,
Trying to remain discreet, ignored.

Dad went to war for a reason,
It wasn't for death, murder or destruction.
It was in the search for an absolute peace,
A place where all fighting had ceased.

Peace is gentle and all-forgiving,
It can create the best of friends where enemies lay.
Peace is a glistening jewel of courage and hope,
Which creates the happiness like a child's Christmas Day.

If you listen carefully
To the air around his grave,
You'll hear it sing of peace and love
Because it knows that one day we might just hear the song across the world.
Never forgotten.

Olivia Vail (13)
Gillotts School, Henley-on-Thames

My Poem About War

The soldiers of England and the soldiers of France, fighting,
Shooting and stabbing with swords, guns firing, soldiers dying,
Planes dropping bombs, but the English won't stop trying.
The sound of the gunshots and the sight of the blood,
Dead bodies and gore, and sometimes a *thud!*

Matthew Palmer (11)
Gillotts School, Henley-on-Thames

War

It is all quiet at home
The only noise I can hear is the kettle
And the doorbell, *ting!*
I'm surrounded by love and laughter.

It is all different in Afghanistan,
In the great, orange plains, the angry sun pierces
My tender skin like a yellow laser beam.
I'm surrounded by death and disaster.

The black, shiny gun is a sad, demented slave.
He is forced to kill, forced to torture,
Forced to be the fear in the back of our minds.
I'm surrounded by death and disaster.

The woeful gunshots rippling angrily through the air
Mingle with the sad cries of death.
The scared dogs bark through the hot and bothered air
I'm surrounded by death and disaster.

Death dances around me, I'm walking in a river of blood.
Bones leave a trail to the valley of unknown
Death is no friend of mine
I'm surrounded by death and disaster.

Two long years later I'm back
But the horrifying memories haunt me.
I will never be at peace.
I'm surrounded by love and laughter
But shadowed by death and disaster.

Connor Wright (14)
Gillotts School, Henley-on-Thames

Poem About War

War is a dreadful time that causes death and sadness.
Most people lose their lives or someone they love.
Destruction and devastation are also what most people feel.
Why did there have to be an awful war?
But none of this would have happened if it wasn't for Hitler!

Patrick Goodrich (11)
Gillotts School, Henley-on-Thames

What Are We Doing To Our World?

The night was once roamed by spectacular creatures
But now has some rather different features,
Where the foxes used to run and play
There is now a motorway, and it's here to stay.

Birds once perched from this very branch
But now there is a chicken ranch,
Soon these poor animals will be eaten
It seems these chickens, by humans, have been beaten.

Animal testing is wrong
In our world, it does not belong.
Animals are tested on and often die
Then discarded, like a week-old pie.

Bang! The elephants run
But they are no match for the huntman's gun.
What happened, what has the world become?

Polar bears, they're in great danger
Their homes are being destroyed by strangers.
The ice that was once here
Is beginning to disappear.

These things need to stop
And you can't just buy that from a shop!
We must work together
Can we ignore this? Never!

Joseph Edwards (11)
Gillotts School, Henley-on-Thames

Fallen Soldier

Standing brave on the front line
With our heads held high
Fighting for our country
Our homes, our lives.

Guns poised,
We're ready to attack,
This is it,
No turning back.

Bang! The first bullet is shot.
Shriek! The first scream is heard.
Crash! The first soldier has fallen.
Thud! The first soldier is dead.

'Emergency! Emergency!
Man down! Man down!'
Doctors try to revive him
But nothing can save him now.

His heart of gold stops beating
A hero forgotten by none.
His devastated parents
Their son will never return.

His fellow soldiers salute him
Their friend is not coming back.
His coffin is going home
Draped in the Union Jack.

Georgia Edwards (14)
Gillotts School, Henley-on-Thames

The World We Live In

Peace, lack of violent conflict
Said so casually, as if there is little inflict
Yet everyone must contradict
And then for me it clicked.

That we may never be at peace
Too many opinions
Too many person personalities
For everyone to disagree.

Actions leading further,
We have created a war
Turning neighbour against neighbour
Door to door.

Weapons down, you wish you hope
If only there could be a vote
But war does not think, nor does it feel
It will not be to your appeal.

Time has passed the war has ended
Yet our pain suspended
Who has remained
We stay afraid.

The news has been told
Hearts broken, young and old
This is war
What else is in store?

Eden Magid (12)
Gillotts School, Henley-on-Thames

Colours

If roses can be red, yellow, pink and white
And still be roses.
If hair can be blonde, brown, white and red
And still be hair.
Then why can't we brown, black, white or pink
And still be people?

Ella D'Souza (12)
Gillotts School, Henley-on-Thames

A Loyal Heart

There are lots of amazing animals throughout the world that roam wild and free
But not all of them can be saved by me.

The food chain stands and poachers are at the top
And *tick-tock* goes the clock.

Night falls and the satisfying sun sinks down into the earth
And another world comes alive at sunrise.

When the lion roars
It roars so loud and full of soul.

With his golden mane
Blowing in the wind
Free with no pain.

As the animals peacefully graze
Bright lights appear form the African haze
Intimidating shadows cast over the path
Tyre tracks and an evil laugh
A silence falls.

Then the lion roars and the animals escape
When a . . . *bang!*

One final roar shutters through the Earth
Painfully it slowly fades
The dripping of a hero's blood slowly stops
And the beating of a loyal heart
Is dead.

Darcy Timms (12)
Gillotts School, Henley-on-Thames

Drugs

D angerous
R idiculous
U nnecessary
G ruesome
S uicidal

Don't take them!

Leilah Lewington (12)
Gillotts School, Henley-on-Thames

Moo Or Money?

The cow is a noble beast.
Respected and honoured by Hindus.
Valued for meat and horn and its Godlike image.
A childhood tradition portrayed in LEGO.
An advertiser's dream for costly creamy cheeses.

Be they black, white, jersey or ginger,
The gentle giants.
Sleeping through the morning mist,
Eyes like calm undisturbed water.
Warm breath moving softly through the fields.
Swishing, swashing tails.
Swish, swash,
Swish, swash.
The cow moos and I marvel, but Man is greedy.

Greedy for burgers greedy for meat, greedy for money.
Ching bling,
Ching bling.

Man has created a meat machine
Spiralling greenhouse gasses
Kyoto ignored and polar bears sinking.
Adorable and gentle or just another way to make money?

Are cows being abused for our greedy needs?
Moo money
Moo money?

Morgan Zolkwer (12)
Gillotts School, Henley-on-Thames

The Consequence Of Bullying

We try and guess why she's crying,
She says she's not but she's lying,
But we can tell that she is.

The next day she's not there,
Miss says not to be scared,
But she killed herself and died.

Josie Day (11)
Gillotts School, Henley-on-Thames

War

War,
Why do we want it?
People are dying, children crying,
It's worthless.

Making holes in the planet.
Destroying people's homes and lives.
Fatherless children left alone.

Crash! Planes go down.
Bang! A gun's been shot.
Boom! A bomb's been dropped.
Whoosh! A missile shoots up into the sky.

The soldiers wait in the cold trenches in fear,
With explosions everywhere they look.
Rats running across the mud,
As planes shooting past deafen their ears.

A never-ending ricochet of bullets bouncing off helmets,
Smoke rises up into the starless sky.

Cities are evacuated, off in trains, still it rains.
With pain in their hearts and tears in their eyes.
Wives waiting to see if their husbands come back,
Or to see the dreaded letter – killed in action.

The soldiers make their way home
Into the cheering crowd of people.

Ben Hodgson (12)
Gillotts School, Henley-on-Thames

The War

One sad morning, a note through the door
To a poor weeping woman soon to weep more.
'Dearest friend, with deepest regret,
I send this letter so you no longer fret.
Your son the bravest, the most revered,
Has tragically died as I'm sure you feared.'

I stand in a trench with my fellow soldiers,
The Germans around us preying like vultures.
The death around us oppressive and heavy
All the work of an elusive Nazi
The screams are awful and the noise is unreal
These scars of battle will never heal.

Then suddenly silence as quickly as it vanished
A thought shared with many the enemy is vanquished!
But, to our horror, as we simply gaze on
We realise the battle has only just begun.
Our soldiers lie, with gazes empty
And we are what is left of the English sentry.

We rise as one to face the enemy,
And risk a glance at England's rugged beauty
Before turning back to the blood-stained battlefield
Knowing ruefully our fate is now sealed.
We stand, weapons raised, proud and tall
Just as the sky begins to fall.

Isobel Greenwood (13)
Gillotts School, Henley-on-Thames

A Mother And Her Son

One sad morning
A mother was mourning
That a revered son had died in the war.
A heart of steel that now was grieving
And so depressed her baby's leaving.
People keep saying he's in a good place
But now she's stuck with an empty space.

Remi Hammant (13)
Gillotts School, Henley-on-Thames

Stop Bullying

'Hey you!'
The boy carried on walking.
'Hey stop!'
The boy stops,
He looks around nervously . . .
'Hey give me your money!'

This a bad start
To something unforgiveable
An upset child.
Stay away, weirdo!
A lonely child.
Do you really want this?

It could change to violence and threat,
It could be a child's worst nightmare.
Being threatened,
Being hurt,
Feeling lonely
Or even feeling like they're on their own planet.

No adult wants to have their child upset.
No one wants to be bullied.
No one wants to deal with it
Or even, no one wants to see it.
Let's stop bullying forever,
Hear it, see it, tell it, *stop it!*

Kate Brooker (11)
Gillotts School, Henley-on-Thames

Sailing

I like sailing on the lake.
The wind rustling against the sails.
Cold wind blowing on my face,
burgee flapping against the wind giving directions.
Clouds scurrying across the sky,
the waves desperately trying to catch up with each other.
Racing across the lake to the smell of warming hot chocolate.

William Primrose (11)
Gillotts School, Henley-on-Thames

Animal Cruelty

Animals are defenceless,
They're also very weak.
What we do to them
Isn't very deep.

How can we replace this evilness
Mend their sore sorrow hearts?
Why is animal cruelty happening?
Why are they being harmed?

Bang goes the birds.
Bang goes the bears.
Smack goes a dog as it fell to the floor from starvation.
Miaow goes the last cat as it dies of diseases.

Splash the last whale surfaced
And tigers are nothing but rugs on the floor.
This should happen no more!

What have they done to us to make our world so cruel?
What have they done to make us do such a thing?
How can people do so wrong?
As they depend on us to look after them.

Sadly animal cruelty is happening all over the world,
Animals dying every day.
They need us so they can stay!
Stop this today and make the world a better place.

Demi Louise Walker (13)
Gillotts School, Henley-on-Thames

The Disaster

The wind whistlers, the waves crack, there's disaster in the air.
The wolves howl by the blowing towel, there's disaster everywhere.
There is no sun, there is no fun disaster isn't fair
Half-beaten houses are full of louse, disaster's in there
The people's hearts are full of dark, disaster's in there.
Then wind blows as the boat rows, disaster's not quite there
The moans and howls as people drown, disaster's everywhere.

Jacob White (11)
Gillotts School, Henley-on-Thames

Unhealthy Eating

It isn't just the greasy fats
The pork pies, fries, the burger buys
That make you so unhealthy.
It's those excess sugars
You know the ones
Glucose, fructose, sucrose
And yes, especially the man-made kind
Disguised as low fat, a labelled lie
But which should state
Eat too much and you die!

Colas, pizzas, crisps and sweets
Are they really all a treat?
They make me giggle and feel more fun
They make me want another one
And another one
I'm young you see, I need to feed my energy.

Then one day they will make you slow
Blood too thick for oxygen to flow.
You're not that old
But cells can't work, insulin is low,
Tumours grow
The gut is putrefying
From the bad foods you've been supplying
You are dying!

Amelia Fielding Smith (12)
Gillotts School, Henley-on-Thames

Bullying

The sound of the trees ruffling
The birds tweeting
The wind blowing
The sound of people rushing
Cars peeping
The sound of the gate opening.

People laughing
People staring
People smiling
People glaring
Opening the classroom door.

People shouting
People calling my name
People being rude
Billy no mates! Billy no mates!
The bell rings.

Sloppy slothy food
With cheesy chocolate drinks
Out on the grassy field
With no mates.

I go home to look at my phone
Hey ugly Betty, hey figgly fatty
Then I cry myself to sleep.

Emily Pitcher (12)
Gillotts School, Henley-on-Thames

My Time To Shine

I've been pushed on stage
The audience await
I'm ready to engage
Ready to begin my fate.

The lights are blinding
Nerves building
As I slowly move over to the mic

I open my mouth
But no words come out
But then I remember my dream.

Being up there with they big stars
Like Ed Sheeran or Jessie J
My name up in big lights
Selling out concerts worldwide.

So I open my mouth
Begin to sing
The words streaming out of my mouth.

So much passion
So much fire
The music takes over me again.

My journey begins, right here, right now
This is my time to shine.

Bronwen Summerwill (13)
Gillotts School, Henley-on-Thames

War

When it's deadlock between two countries
And a bullet makes it all start
With one side and another attacking each other
On two fronts or maybe more
With technology or without
Only one side will win
Who will it be?

The fields or the cities
They will both be in it
Import ships being destroyed
Food on the decrease
The farmers having to make as much food as possible
To keep the families from starving
Feeding everyone for years to come.

Bangs of guns
Bangs from explosions
Injuries unable to treat
Young men
Old men
Middle aged men
Getting killed in thick of the action.

Will it end soon?
No one knows!

Will Poray (13)
Gillotts School, Henley-on-Thames

Smoking

Stale smoke
Yellow fingers
Wheezing lungs
Stained teeth
Suffocating slowly
Wrinkly skin
Bad breath
Smoking kills.

Will Emerson (14)
Gillotts School, Henley-on-Thames

War

War is scary,
War is *war!*
It makes you mourn
Those loved before.

They may be dead
But they're still in your head
So don't wriggle around in your bed
Because you know they're dead.

The man was brave
And there he lay
Unable to move no more.

He protected the land
Controlled by Man
For people he loves no more.

This man was shot
By a terrible plot
A bullet in his head
For the bravery he shared
That Man will always be loved.

So take this note
As a warning to vote
That war should happen no more.

Jamie Olive & Jack Patterson (13)
Gillotts School, Henley-on-Thames

Racism

Discriminated,
Unregulated,
Unjustified.
Racism is a crime.
The streets are lined with masked attackers
Buoyant in their excitement to hurl abuse at another race.
But why?
Because they're different.

Jordan Poulos (13)
Gillotts School, Henley-on-Thames

Survival

Before we lived animals wandered like kings
We often wonder what then was living
Did we come along and knock them off their throne?
Large and small, all kinds of animals roamed

Did they ever know that we would rise to remove their pride?
Hunters galore make them run and hide
Now that so many of their species are dying out
Let's stand up and hear them shout

Many a man likes to run and chase
The animals try to pick up pace
Some get caught, some get away
I will never hurt them, not tomorrow, not today

Several leopards are killed every day
Killed for their skins, no more will they play
My ideal would be to let them live
Do their pack really forget and forgive?

Just like us animals are living too
Is it OK that some are made into stew
Stop it now they don't need to be killed
Come on humans, where's the thrill?

Killing animals really is absurd
I wish animals had a voice to be heard.

Harrison Kirkwood (11)
Gillotts School, Henley-on-Thames

The War

All the people in the war
People getting injured, people dying
And with my dad left to go it made me very sad.
On my 11th birthday, he wasn't there.
On my 12th birthday he wasn't there.
On my 13th birthday he wasn't there.
On my 14th birthday he wasn't there
On my 15th birthday my mum said he died and then I cried and cried.

Sallie Ann Wheeler (12)
Gillotts School, Henley-on-Thames

The Bully Should Always Regret

It's just a laugh; it's just a game
I didn't mean to bring her pain.
I pushed and shoved from side to side,
I guess that built the emotion slide.
Falling, falling, down, down, down,
Until she stopped and hit the ground.
We all just laughed and ran away
And we never saw her the next day.

In she came a few days later,
Limp, limp, limp, what a faker!
She looked at us and started to cry,
She tried to leave, just walk on by.
We caught her up and stopped her tracks,
She tried to slip behind our backs.

That's it fatty, big fat bubble,
You tried to get us into trouble.
Let this be your warning, we're after you
And there is nothing you can do!

She just stood up and moved right back,
She pulled out something from her pack.
She lifted it forward and said goodbye.

Kayleigh Isaac (13)
Gillotts School, Henley-on-Thames

Untitled

Poor dogs lying on the streets
Tiny kittens being abused
Nothing is left for them to eat
They're all so confused.

Animal testing
This is so wrong
Why is no one protesting?
All animals will be gone.

Zoe Smith (12)
Gillotts School, Henley-on-Thames

Dying For Change

Many human beings settle on designing tables and charts
But a few relish the gruesome task of shooting poison darts.

Some clever humans face our world very dangerous knowledge
Man never had this problem, when he was back at college.

Overfishing, poaching and hunting each species to its end
These helpless creatures run and hide but are unable to defend.

When will this 21st Century madness ever decrease?
Every day the number rise and the killings never cease.

All animals now run scared; unaware of what is their fate
Remember; be careful when you order, what might be upon your plate!

Man is a heartless fool to continue killing hour by hour,
Leaving Mother Nature little time to recover and flower.

Why can't these nasty people learn to live together?
Alongside all of god's creatures fish, fur and feather.

Many poachers kill for sport but never stop to understand
Soon there will be nothing left but you and me upon this land.

Time will never be a healer, already there is too much to regret
Now extinct, a number of them, memories in books I won't forget.

So next time you buy some clothing or some furniture for a treat,
Remember you could be buying the last one that stood upon its own four feet!

Nico Cheesman (12)
Gillotts School, Henley-on-Thames

The Bully

I never understood why
I let it go to my mind
The hurt that the words brought
The words became my every thought.

Bang, bang went the gun
I remember hearing when I was young
The bullet came out of his mouth
It shot me straight in the heart from the south.

Sophie Ashton (13)
Gillotts School, Henley-on-Thames

Cause And Casuality

There was a man,
A simple man,
A man with an infinite world to explore
With infinite possibilities
A world of beauty.

As the man grew clever he mapped the world
Building cities and towns.
But as he built more and more he had less and less
Beauty and resources depleted
Hills and mountains for factories and mines.

Until nothing
Nothing left at all
The man transcended
Fitting all odds, avoiding meteors, solar storms,
Pulsars and exploding suns.
Only to be destroyed by himself
Transcending to glory and knowledge
Yet sinking into his own quicksand
Building more and more, sinking more and more
Extinction on a massive scale
To the penultimate downfall of the old man
To the penultimate downfall of the human race
Think!

Rupert Wiseman (13)
Gillotts School, Henley-on-Thames

The War That Never Ends

Wherever there is man there is war, why is this?
Is it because we thirst for power
Or is it because we like to see another man's blood run?
Bang! Another gunshot, another man dead, another widow weeping.
This is not how it should be, life is a great thing that is so simple
But yet so fragile and it is at its breaking point.

'Tomorrow is a mystery, yesterday was history
And today is a gift, that is why it is called the present.'

Oscar James (11)
Gillotts School, Henley-on-Thames

Hurricane Katrina

Katrina, Katrina your name sounds so calm
Whoever believed you could cause so much harm.
You hurtled your way past the seas
Reducing New Orleans to its knees.

Katrina, Katrina I bet you had so much fun
Causing mayhem and destruction in your run
Bodies were floating down the river
You are the life taker, not the giver.

Katrina, Katina, so much lives in danger,
Where was God that day, was He a stranger?
Winds were blowing down remnants of a road
Taking giant steps you roared as you strode.

You sucked up the trees like a Hoover
No one could run, cars could not manoeuvre
You blew down tin roofs, houses and cars
Strutting down the streets like an asteroid from Mars
Katrina, Katrina, you destroyed all in your path
High up in the atmosphere, you had the last laugh.

America, America you are the land of the brave
When it comes to the money too bad you couldn't save
America, America you spend so much money putting junk in your mouth
Where are your dollars to rebuild New Orleans the pride of the South?

Danny Clifford (12)
Gillotts School, Henley-on-Thames

Drinking

D rinking is fun, I love it
R emembering nothing the next day, I love it
I then realise what I have done, I hate it
N ow I can't drink again, I hate it
K nowing I'm an alcoholic, I hate it
I now can't help but drink, I hate it
N ow I regret going too far with alcohol
G etting too much alcohol is something I don't recommend, don't do it!

Callum Reeves (13)
Gillotts School, Henley-on-Thames

War

It all started over the turning of the car
The car which went the wrong way
The car which was carrying a duke
The car which was carrying an accident waiting to happen.

He was a good man, he meant no harm
But when he was shot, it all fired up
The life of men changed as they voted themselves up
They had no choice, for country, for wife, for victory
But they had no idea what was in store for them.

From the training camp they saw the glow of war
But the worst was still to come
Two weeks had passed; they were walking to the front line
To disease, to gunfire, to probably death
That walk would change their lives
There were thirty of them how many would come back?

Two days gone, ten deaths already, how many in four?
The constant noise as if the haves were screaming
But one day it would end
There would be nothing of battlefields
Nothing of trenches, nothing of war
That is when peace will arrive
And people will be able to live without fear.

Harry Saunders (13)
Gillotts School, Henley-on-Thames

Bully

The pain that hurts, the tears that cry
All the pain I've suffered by
You push me and poke me
But I guarantee
That's enough playing with me
I go to school
Where you stop and laugh at me
I don't know what I've done; I'm innocent as I can be
Let me be free.

Molly Lambourne (14)
Gillotts School, Henley-on-Thames

Always Look

They had the right to drive
It happened to my dog
There was no fog
They could see very clearly
It was not just them
To me it tastes like lime . . . all sour
Why did you not get punished?
It really was not fair
If you looked my dog would be happy
And so would my family
She was my life, I loved her
That was my life too!
So who are you?
It makes me wonder
You should be careful next time
Because that was a crime
I was six
But it can't be fixed
This broke my heart
And you are never to e seen again
So why really, just why
It's ended, it's over
But not for me!

Holley O'Fiera (11)
Gillotts School, Henley-on-Thames

This Is War

War, in the trenches.
Should this really be?
Sacred faces all around me.
Is this the place for me?

Bullets flying, people dying.
Is this problem being solved.
Or is it becoming another?
At the end it won't be either.
This is war.

Adam Strickson (13)
Gillotts School, Henley-on-Thames

The Explosion

A flash
A blinding light
A growing bulge on the horizon
A *smash,* a thud
A *whoosh* of air.
The ground buckles and cracks.
A screaming woman clutched her child
A child with so much to see his journey cut short by a feud.
The *smash* of breaking glass.
The *whine* of car alarms.
The heat grows the light brightens.
The thwack as a shard of glass embeds itself into the woman's chest.
The shriek of the helpless child.
The last gasp from the woman's punctured lungs.
The building crackles, I saw it fall.
It buried him alive!
His mangled body mixed in the blood of his mother.
Yet another victim of a stupid war.
Suddenly my body gave in,
I felt my last breath and my beat.
I collapsed my body left to rot.
I was just another expendable human.
Never to be thought of, never cared for and never to be remembered.

Matthew Powell (12)
Gillotts School, Henley-on-Thames

War

Wars can be started in many ways,
Some soldiers survive for only a few days.
Families are broken,
Riflemen are woken,
By the sound of the shooting raid.

Bombs falling form the skies as the helicopters zoom overhead.
Millions and millions of helpless civilians lay there dead.
The war keeps raging on without an end in sight.
People who sit and wait whish there was not a fight.

Joseph Nichols (12)
Gillotts School, Henley-on-Thames

Stop Bullying!

I stood there helpless
There was nothing I could say
I watched like a spectator
Like I'd done for half the day.

I opened my mouth
But the words didn't come out
I wanted to help
But my mouth was like a drought.

I stared at my friend
Being beaten up
When would it end?

He was screaming in pain
And I couldn't contain my shame
Bullying makes you feel bad
You come home and you feel sad.
No one ever deals with it
With your help, we could stop it a little bit.

Bullying is so bad
I can't contain my frustration
Put a stop to bullying
And save the nation.

Ben Porter (12)
Gillotts School, Henley-on-Thames

Poem About War

As soldiers march into war
One gets shot as bullets fall
Enemies hide behind a wall
Explosion goes. They're there no more
Planes they scrape the sky
Tanks they drive by.

Bang! A bullet is shot.
Slash! A knife is drawn.
Boom! The war is over.

Ben Daniels (11)
Gillotts School, Henley-on-Thames

Global Warming

As devastating as it is
Global warming exists!
Ice melting worldwide
Tides swept aside.

Our impressive home, she's crying
Penetrated with a thousand rays of sun.

Your atmosphere demolished
Like a construction plummeting towards the bottom.

Suddenly, obscure seabed vanishes
Mystical fish no home
Their seabed's destroyed by Man's arrogance.

Broom, broom, the cars slither down the destructive road
Fumes pierce the lung of the world
They surround us.

Trees stolen, animals gone
Nature is destroyed,
What will we do when the world is gone?

Stop global warming
Fight for your land
Together the world will understand!

Nadia Shalini Sherlock (13)
Gillotts School, Henley-on-Thames

Stop Bullying!

Bullying is bad; you think it's good
You made them cry as you thought you would.

You should know, bullying hurts.
It starts with one word, one word you blurt.
Fat, ugly, worthless, these are the words they hear
Did you know you're their biggest fear?

It takes so long for their hearts to mend
All they ask for is one true friend
But you make them want their lives to end.

Holly Verran (11)
Gillotts School, Henley-on-Thames

Look At Her!

Look at her
She is perfect.
Her eyes,
Her nose,
Her teeth,
Her lips, perfect.

Look at her
Sitting by the pool
With her perfect tan
And cute little fan.

Look at her,
Just look.
Look at her,
Now look at me.

Look at me,
I'm not perfect.
My teeth are wonky
My nose is crooked
My hair is thin and ratty
I'm not perfect
But that's just me!

Josie Watts (12)
Gillotts School, Henley-on-Thames

I Won't Give Up

It's the same every day, the same name,
The same place with the same nasty disapproving faces.
They all chant loud with their ice cold voices
On the outside I take it but on the inside I ache of sadness.
It could all be over with one simple decision
But that would be giving up before I'd even tried wouldn't it?
I will stop the names that make me shame.
I will stop them laughing in my face.
I'm not going to give up,
I won't.

Amber Pocock (14)
Gillotts School, Henley-on-Thames

Stop Smoking

Smoking is an addiction
Smoking is a drug
Please give it up
It will kill your lungs

Every single day
People die in pain
From the smoking chain.

The adults are dying
The children are crying,
Crying.

I walk down the street
I see people smoking
They're killing themselves
Without even knowing.

Whether it's
1, 2, or 80 a day
People still die
In the cruellest way.

Stop it, stop it, stop it now
Because smoking is really foul!

Tyler Reed (12)
Gillotts School, Henley-on-Thames

My Life

My shoes, my trousers my top, my colour
All of these things change the minds of others.
Everyone judges from day to day
But today will be my day.
Did anyone expect me to be doing
Ballet dance or croquet?
I walk down the street every day
My insides twist a people look always.
The outside they ear but the inside of me
Is something they just don't see.

Sam Verran (13)
Gillotts School, Henley-on-Thames

There's Nowhere To Hide

Screens, screams
The phone yelps
You can't run away
There's nowhere to hide.

Hiding, hiding
Away for this nightmare
Soon finding
There's nowhere to hide.

Crying, crying
A digital attack
Unable to fight
There's nowhere to hide.

Sadness, sadness
Tears up the night
Someone has a heart of stone
There's nowhere to hide.

You feel alone
You don't know who to tell
Worried and anxious
There's nowhere to hide.

Romilly Hryczanek (13)
Gillotts School, Henley-on-Thames

War . . . What Is It Good For?

As the gunshells fall
And the bodies drop,
Hope and happiness turns to despair
Countless lives lost for what
As families hope for their loved ones
And pray they will live!
What hope do we have?

Why
For what
Why?

William Properjohn (12)
Gillotts School, Henley-on-Thames

Halloween Is Coming

Ten carved pumpkins
Glowing in the dark.
Nine Halloween monsters
Lurking in the park.

Eight colourful candles,
Orange, yellow and white.
Seven ghastly ghosts
Giving everyone a fright.

Six scary spiders,
Their webs complete.
Five cheeky children
Going to trick or treat.

Four wicked witches
Stirring up a brew.
Three black cats
Part of their crew.

Two big bats
Flying higher and higher.
One full moon
As bright as a fire.

Zara Hawkins (11)
Gillotts School, Henley-on-Thames

War

The final trigger for the final man
His heart beats bigger as he ran.
A bomb goes off on the nearby ground
The bang and the cries just a normal sound.
Bits of wire and scrap clawing at his feet
His feet pounds fast, in time with his heartbeat.
Boom! Another squad down.
Smash! Another man dead.
At last he sees his camp south of Dover
A sudden *bang* and it was all over.

Amy Tillyer (11)
Gillotts School, Henley-on-Thames

You Think?

You think I'm this,
You think I'm that,
Stupid, slow and scummy
Don't judge me 'cause I'm fat.

You think I'm this,
You think I'm that,
Anorexic, arrogant and apathetic
I've been labelled a brat.

You think I'm this,
You think I'm that,
Hazardous hooded hooligans
A dangerous prat.

You think I'm this,
You think I'm that,
Dork, dweeb, dolt
Just 'cause I did well in my SAT.

If you had not judged us so
You might have really got to know
And maybe even been our friend
But you chose to stereotype instead.

Stephanie Croft & Jemima Pilgrim-Morris (13)
Gillotts School, Henley-on-Thames

My Maths Class Is Like A Zoo

'This class is a zoo,' the maths teacher said,
'3 is a sloth who is still in bed.
5 is like a monkey, cunning and quick and
7 is as sharp as an eagle's beak.
11 is crawling under the desk and
13 is beating a tune on his chest.
17 is camouflaged to get out of work, but
19 has climbed to a higher perch
And that's just the primes,' she said with awe
And with a flourish she went out the door.

Oliver Gann (14)
Gillotts School, Henley-on-Thames

The Senses Of A War Poem

The sights of war are evil
Damage, destruction, death.
Trenches, shells, guns,
Colours of war, black, red with blood on earth.

The sounds of war are ear-splitting
Explosions of bombs, machine guns, *yak yak!*
Shouting, sobbing, yelling,
Drones of aeroplanes screaming of shells.

The touch of war is harsh
Aeroplanes soaring high, bullets booming below.
Metal, flesh, mud,
Earth flying carelessly around.

The taste of war is defeat
Despair in the air, bitter all around.
Smoke, dirt, dust,
Filthy water, musty air.

The smell of war is fear,
The stench of rotting bodies, pollution all around.
Gunpowder, burning sewage,
The lurking smell of gas.

Caitlin Copland (13)
Gillotts School, Henley-on-Thames

Smoking!

I watch her
I watch her
I watch her inhale
The deadly black cloud that would slowly sail
She stops, she stares, before my eyes
The smoke which did drift up to the skies
Every breath I take was feeling
Like I had been heavily drinking
I hope when she sees my scared, anxious face
She will stop this deadly drug and make me safe.

Chloe Oswald (14)
Gillotts School, Henley-on-Thames

The Bang

The bang, the pain
The loss, the gain
Why should the world end this way?

We shouldn't fight
We should love
The whole world should be as one.

The land should join, the whole world should have fun
When people are out all through the night
Ready to cry, ready to fight.

We need to be strong
We need to be fast
We need to end up on top.

And if we don't
We'll lose it all
The world, the love
And all of the fun.

People cower in corners
Extremely scared
Wondering why it has to be them.

Adam Bellman (12)
Gillotts School, Henley-on-Thames

Stop Smoking

Do you think that smoking is good for you?
Then you do not have a clue.
Smoking can make you lose your life
And damage your lungs like a knife.

It costs a lot of money
Which is not very funny.

It clings to you and makes you smell
Like the fiery depths of Hell!

It does not just hurt you
But also those who love you!

Sophie McLaren (13)
Gillotts School, Henley-on-Thames

Global Warming

As the ice caps melt
Into a sea of doubt,
There's no more hiding from the sun
As the consumer buys
And the landscape dies
Is it too late to reverse what has begun?
As we over-fish
For our favourite dish
Was it our right to take it all?
As we unite to fail
Under the vapour trail
Did we run before we could crawl?
Are we running out of space?
For the human race?
Is there anywhere we haven't been?
As the teardrops rise
With the turning tide
But the water's still polluted in the stream
So the ice caps melt
Into a sea of doubt
And we just lay there in the sun.

Leoni Hughes (13)
Gillotts School, Henley-on-Thames

Untitled

The war zone was empty,
Most of the enemy had fled, many were dead.
The sound of weapons constantly firing
Bang! Bang!
Had vanished into the freezing cold air.
So quiet, no enemy to be seen.
'Enemy!' screamed the look out.
Thud! He had been hit,
Lost his life for nothing.
More than some disgusting bread.
Then I asked myself, 'Why are we doing this?'

Carl Webb (13)
Gillotts School, Henley-on-Thames

Glorious Food

I'm going to have a muffin or two
Maybe I'll have a burger with you.
However, I could have fish and chips
It all sounds yummy; I'm licking my lips.

The muffins were delicious
(One is never enough)
The inside is filled with squidgy chocolate stuff.

The burger was fantastic
A super-duper triple mac.
Meat and cheese and mayonnaise
All in one big greasy stack.

The fish was wrapped in batter
The chips were cooked in fat.
The grease dribbles down the chin
And I love it just like that!

No! I can't go running
And I can't go on a hike
And now my bottom's way too fat
To even fit on my bike!

Oscar Rait (11)
Gillotts School, Henley-on-Thames

War

War! War! People actually want more
As the planes fly in and men dying.
Bang, the next gun is shot.
Bang, another man is dead.
Bang, the next bomb has blown up.
As you're in your cabin all battered from training
You know what's coming next
Soon you will be dying in a muddy ditch.
War! War! People actually want more.
You're running in all next to war.
War! War! Everybody hates war.

Marshall Stanbridge Bennett (11)
Gillotts School, Henley-on-Thames

The Rabbit's Lament

(Dedicated to Fluffy)

Your loss gave me pain and doubt
A heartbreak not meant
One I could've done without
But your last day spent.

I should've done something
Said something
But not a word
Not a sound
Came out
A tear just trickled down and down.

The soil will keep you warm my dear
No more thoughts of fear
In your bed my dear
As forget-me-nots blanket your ears.

'My dear sweet rabbit,' I whisper,
'Twas not your time at all
Your life is now complete
But I haven't said goodbye at all.

Sophie Wermann (13)
Gillotts School, Henley-on-Thames

Untitled

The streets have been dirtied
The oceans are black
Where is Mother Nature,
Please can you come back.

Fish are all choking
And yet no one cares
The Earth so mighty just sits and despairs.

Clank another can gets dropped
Crack another bottle is smashed
Thud birds seem obsolete
I just want the world to go back to being neat.

Ieuan Price-Davies (12)
Gillotts School, Henley-on-Thames

War

You hear the crashing and smashing
You run out of your house and turn to see
The big devourer is heading straight towards you
Crushing and treading down everything in its wake.

You run like crazy as fast as you can
Behind the devourer dust and ruins are left
People lie motionless on the ground crushed in the jaws of the beast
Some have been wounded, their legs caught under trees and houses.
You keep going and catch a glimpse of another, strong and fierce and frightening.
It looks a little different from the other
But still leaves nothing behind.

As the two collide, people are crushed, houses are brought down
There is wreckage everywhere and the two beasts leave shortly.

We are left with nothing but emptiness
Everything we once knew is gone
And now we are left to pick ourselves up and start anew.
That is what war leaves for us, what does it leave for you?

Arran Campbell (13)
Gillotts School, Henley-on-Thames

Bullies

Respect one another
As you would your brother.

In Year 5 I had a bad time
Folks picking on me really was a crime.

How do you deal with it?

It wrecks your day
You feel like suffocating in some hay.

It wears you down
Right to the ground.

Respect one another
As you would your brother.

Felix Ratcliffe (11)
Gillotts School, Henley-on-Thames

Smoking!

Smoking, smoking, why are people such fools?
Smoking, smoking, they don't need to do it at all.

I hate it,
It's just paper lit
Why is it such a habit?

People are buying cigarettes and then burning their money.
I don't think it's good and I don't think it's funny.

Your lungs suffer the consequence,
Do you want to die?
I didn't think so,
So why do you do it, oh why?

In case I didn't say it clearly.
Smoking is bad
So drop those cigarettes out of your hand.

Imagine how worried your family are.
So say stop before it's too late
Smoking kills, so don't make that mistake.

Elise Jordan Reed (11)
Gillotts School, Henley-on-Thames

War

What is the point in war?
Devastation everywhere
Buildings turned to rubble
Bombs dropping from the air.

A battlefield once a spring meadow
Now a graveyard for the dead
Loved ones never to return
Broken promises after all that was said.

The sky illuminated showing a red river
Smells of sulphur raising from the floor
The cries of pain and suffering
What is the point in war?

Olivia Sims (12)
Gillotts School, Henley-on-Thames

We All Belong

I'm fed up from feeling all this pain
Everyone acts like it's a game.
The names. They stick in my brain.
I felt like no one understood.
Then one day, it only took one name
For me to feel like I needed to suffer more pain.
It escalated. I wanted to die
And that's when I tried to commit suicide.
I never thought I'd be in the position
Where I felt like I belonged in a mental institution.
It felt like there was no way out
And on the inside all I could do was shout.
They don't realise how much it hurts
To think of yourself as a piece of dirt
Letting people walk all over you.
At the end of the day we are who we are
No one should feel like they don't belong
So remember God made us to be as one
And that everyone belongs.

Stacey Griffin (13)
Gillotts School, Henley-on-Thames

21st Century

Stuck in their rooms
Nowhere to run
Joblessness looms
Technology is their second mum.

Dreams are unreal
Future is dim
No room for errors
Or you have to face your sins.

Whoosh! Goes nature
Boom! Goes reality
Left is technology
Sitting there happily.

Saphi Hancock (12)
Gillotts School, Henley-on-Thames

Deforestation

Don't cut down the trees
Eventually there'll be none left
For every animal will lose their life
Orang-utans, monkeys, jaguars and frogs
Rubber trees are cut down every day
Everyone who does it has no heart
So if you ever see it you better make a stand
The rainforest will be gone
And we'll soon follow
Those poor animals that we will never see again
If anyone's job is cutting down trees
They are making money which they haven't earned
Old history lies with the rainforest
Nothing should stop it from being a future landmark.

Emil Rayfield (11)
Gillotts School, Henley-on-Thames

What Shall I Do Now?

Lying here so still and livid
Hands so cold no sight of the sun
Face like a morning never to come
What shall I do now?

Like a shadow standing loomingly there
Running into pick a family to tear
What can I do now?

I run away, no love can cure him ever
I remember his laugh and the fun we had together
What will I do now?

Cancer will kill, cancer will ruin
Cancer is the disease Mother
That has taken life from my beloved brother

Emma Dodd (12)
Gillotts School, Henley-on-Thames

Growing Older

Getting ready to say goodbye
Ready to begin a new journey
Of being way up high
Without all of the worries or cares
I'm up in the skies and I miss you
Never forget me
Getting ready to meet someone new.

Oh how I wish I was still there
Loving you with my tender care
Don't worry about me, I'll be fine
Ever yours my valentine
Remember all the good times not the bad
Because I don't want to think of you being sad.

Ella Morgan (13)
Gillotts School, Henley-on-Thames

War

It all starts with a bullet
The bang of a gun
The loss of a life
A war to be won.

How many left
How many gone
War has fallen
The battle has begun.

Driven by hatred
Driven by greed
Driven by trust
Driven by lust.

Seasons come and go
The war is never ending
The sky is black
The rivers red
Hell and Earth are blending.

Marcus Pike (13)
Gillotts School, Henley-on-Thames

Ash Rains Down On This Empty Town

Ash rains down on this empty town
From the crashing and the burning
What has this world come to now?

Each day I wonder
Could I have helped?
Would I have helped?
Instead I only ponder.

Bang! Bang!
Goes the sound of a rifle
Like screaming in my ears.
The bombs are like mini earthquakes
I can only watch as they grow near.

This is the world I grow up in
The bombsites are my playground now
I miss all my friends and family
As the ash rains down on this empty town.

Katie Thompson (14)
Gillotts School, Henley-on-Thames

Global Warming

G lass is burning
L itres of petrol in the atmosphere
O ver years the ice has disappeared
B lasts of smoke released
A ntarctica has gone
L ove your environment.

W hales are struggling to breathe
A nts can't hide anymore
R eevving of the engines
M otors releasing gas
I nk released into the sea
N ever leave a car running
G as burning the atmosphere.

Samuel Baker (12)
Gillotts School, Henley-on-Thames

The Cat

Marbles the cat
Who has ears like a bat
The one with the scent
Who can sniff out the rat.

His long bushy tail
Providing a trail in the soft white snow
His blackness stands out
His whiskers about, his paws seem to endlessly grow.

His eyes widen bright
As they follow the red kite
His eyes flicker in the night
From the shimmering light.

He stretches out straight
In front of the gate
Waiting for the fishermen's bait
At the end of the day, he's only a stray
And there's nothing that I can do to turn him away.

Freddie Fox-Wilson (11)
Gillotts School, Henley-on-Thames

Put A Stop To Bullying

Put a stop to bullying
On that we all agree.
All bullies are insecure at heart
As everyone can see.
When being bullied and inside you want to cry
Just show them that you really don't care
And hold your head up high.
Bullying can be verbal or on the Internet online
Physical is also just as bad
And you have bruising as a sign.
So put a stop to bullying
And make the world a better place.
Stand up to all these cowards and put a smile upon your face
Beat bullying and be bold.

Sam Williams (12)
Gillotts School, Henley-on-Thames

Global Warming

A hundred years of CO2
No wonder we'll kill Earth so soon.
Animals will die and we will too,
If we don't stop our human zoo.

Our so-called civilisation
Will destroy our worldwide nation
If we don't stop this man-made creation
There will be no future for Earth's children.

Our climate is changing
Ice caps are melting
Global warming has caught us snoring
We must start restoring our beloved Earth.

Climate change is everyone's problem
We can't ignore this
We all can do something for Mother Earth
Join the worldwide cause and save our Earth
Just remember there's no planet B.

Merlin Hempshall (11)
Gillotts School, Henley-on-Thames

War

Keeping his body perfectly still, waiting for the signal to go,
Watching . . . waiting . . . listening.
He waits in silence not wanting anyone to hear,
Watching . . . waiting . . . listening.
Loading his rifle, his bayonet ready to thrust,
Watching . . . waiting . . . listening.
He is ready but still he fears,
Watching . . . waiting . . . listening.
As the signal sounds, out of the trenches he climbs,
Watching . . . listening.
With his gun at the ready, *bang!* Gunshots are heard,
But not for long.
No one alive to watch . . . wait or listen.
Silence descends.

Maisie Webb (14)
Gillotts School, Henley-on-Thames

All The Stuff That Is Bad About War

War is bad
It is quite sad
Lots of people die
I don't know why
Because there is no reason for them to die.

Blood, guts and gore
All over the floor
Oh what a mess is war!

Hitler was the worst of all
He was obviously quite a fool
Because he started World War II
And he was a Nazi too.

The V2 bomb was quite a scare
So much so people hid under the stair
I'm just glad I wasn't there.

Max Wermann (11)
Gillotts School, Henley-on-Thames

War Worth Fighting For?

See that man over there
He fought in war and he fought fair.
So just don't mistake him for some old man
Thanks to him you live the way you can.

Normal people under fire
All the terrorists desire.
Women, men and children dead
All their blood a racing red.

This is war
A soldier's chore.
Their families cry
As the soldiers die.

War – is it worth fighting for?

Julia Bernat (12)
Gillotts School, Henley-on-Thames

Abandoned

Watching the children come out to play
Screaming and shouting, hooray, hooray!
But there he lay
Through night and day.

Abandoned by his friend
He had nowhere to sleep
Nothing to eat
Where could he be, where?

People would stare
People would scream
But only he had lost his dream.

As he sat there
He watched his old lawn
Where he was born
Where his heart was torn.

The dog, a man's best friend.

Katie Tillyer (12)
Gillotts School, Henley-on-Thames

War

Smoke hangs upon the air, the dead are on the ground.
Cries of pain fill the sky and blood is all around.
My soldiers are in the trenches with the enemy up in front.
My friends are getting shot, again we take the brunt.

Why, I must ask myself,
Why do we have to fight?
Why must Man fight himself
And set our land alight?

The time for killing is over
And death has claimed its fill.
Was it really worth it,
Did blood need to spill?

Luke Heppenstall (14)
Gillotts School, Henley-on-Thames

Peer Pressure

Peer pressure always getting you down
You don't want to do what they say.
Peer pressure always getting you down
If you don't toe the line you'll look like a clown.

Peer pressure always getting you down
Wear the right clothes when we meet in town.
Peer pressure always getting you down
Like what we like or you'll be on your own.

Peer pressure always getting you down
Afraid to say no and be shunned from the crowd.
Peer pressure always getting you down
Brave to seek help but too scared you'll regret it.

Peer pressure always getting you down
One day I'll beat them and stand tall and proud.
Peer pressure, never getting me down
I know who I am and I'll shout it out loud!

Maisie Edwards (12)
Gillotts School, Henley-on-Thames

Bullying

The circus master is in the girls' toilets
She raises her whip
Because she is as cruel as a witch.
The victim is sad and is full of hate
She wishes it wouldn't be this way
But the circus master is tough
And powerful like a gorilla
Who swings her arms and pushes the girl.
The girl bleeds and can't cope anymore
She goes to the exit but the master's gang comes
And pushes her back.
At night she doesn't need to hide behind her smile
You wouldn't like to be this girl
So tell someone, it *will* stop!

Leila Summers (12)
Gillotts School, Henley-on-Thames

The Media Vs Me

The media makes me sound bad,
The media is what makes me sad.
The public think the media is true,
They all really don't have a clue.

Apple juice is what I drink,
Alcohol is what the media think.
Smoking is what the media say I do,
They all really don't have a clue.

Bunking is what the media says,
Failing is what the media displays.
But homework is what I do,
They all really don't have a clue.

I wish they got it right,
I wish they brought the good things to light.
Getting it wrong, that's what they do
Do they all think they have a clue?

Izzy Narracott (14)
Gillotts School, Henley-on-Thames

Destruction

What's happening to the modern world?
The idea of inventiveness has just been hurled.
What is real fun?
Seems now it's just playing with a gun,
The young child's mind focused on getting to the next level
On an Xbox or PS3.

Thump, another tree hacked down,
Just for roll to clean up our mess,
Isn't this a sign for our major distress?

No more animals to be amazed by,
No lovely scenery to look and wonder at,
Is this really saving for the next generation?

Dominic Meeks (11)
Gillotts School, Henley-on-Thames

Salmon Farming

An empty river
Where salmon once swam
Alive and free
To travel up river and down.

Born to swim
To hunt
To be salmon.

But all their freedom
Confined to a cage
Placed high and wide
Just to feed a nation.

Sprayed and fed chemicals
That poison the bed below
For a fiver at Morrisons or Tesco.

How would you like to be trapped in the thousands with one fate
To be placed on a plate?

Rosie Fort (12)
Gillotts School, Henley-on-Thames

War

Everyone is the same; it's not a game.
War is wrong! Are there people to blame?
Stop pretending ,it's never-ending.
People are dying, barely anyone surviving.

What happens if Daddy doesn't come home today?
Well, then there will be arrangements made!
No summer days? No more happy, Daddy days?
I just wish he could have stayed.

Oh Daddy, my prayers never came true,
I must have been a bad girl for you!
Don't worry; I will fight for me and Mummy.

I will grow up and greet you, one day you will see
That you will be so proud of me!

Sara Barrett (13)
Gillotts School, Henley-on-Thames

Anti-Smoking!

Smoke now with no affect
Deadly poison your lungs detect.
It's something that can kill you
It's slow and calm
But it really does harm!

You think it's cool, you think it's fun
To put your lips upon a cigarette
But that you will regret.

Your lungs are filled with deadly smoke
The people around you have no choice
Than to breathe in and choke
Upon your offensive, selfish smoke!

So now it's time to give it all up
You know it's the right thing to do.
You will save yourself
And those around you.

Ella Roullier (11)
Gillotts School, Henley-on-Thames

Cancer

People crying, people dying,
People coming, people going,
Who deserves this?
No one!
Who can help?
Everyone!
Save their grief, save their loss,
Save their families, save their choice.
They have feelings as well,
Let's try to make their lives swell.
They have families too,
So let's give them a clue.
How to have a great life,
No crying, no dying,
No coming, no going.

Kerry Allum (12)
Gillotts School, Henley-on-Thames

War Is A Waste

Your brain is an amazing thing.
Planning, inventing, designing, creating
Endless possibilities of what you can do.
Why use it to create machines of war
When you could make the world a better place?

Your body is a cool thing.
Running, jumping, moving, helping
The world is your oyster.
Why use your body to fight and do harm
When you could make the world a better place?

The world's resources are a fantastic gift.
Providing warmth, shelter and food
War is a waste of resources and time
But even more a waste of precious life.

Matthew Gavin (13)
Gillotts School, Henley-on-Thames

War

War is there any end
To this world affair?
Hearts broken, unable to mend.
Everyone sits waiting, showing their care.

Lives stand still
For those who are still wishing
That maybe they will come back
Not condemned missing.

They do a great thing
For me, for you.
Will one day the birds all sing?
That at last the angels have guided them through.

It's a funny thing 'war'
But not funny ha-ha
We all need a little bit more
Peace.

Megan Ritson (14)
Gillotts School, Henley-on-Thames

Poaching

The animals are going,
Falling like pins
But by whose doing?
Who is committing such sins?

Poaching is evil,
Poaching is cruel,
Poaching is wrong.
A poacher is a fool.

No tigers are left,
No crocodiles at all.
The rainforest are bereft
The consequence is tall.

Poaching has struck.
The animals are dead.
It was not bad luck,
It was greed, instead.

Joshua Mill (11)
Gillotts School, Henley-on-Thames

Racism - Does It Matter

Does it really matter if you're tall?
Does it really matter if you're small?
Does it really matter if you're black?
Does it really matter if you're white?

All that matters is you!
It doesn't matter at all if your skin is a different colour,
All that matters is you!

Don't let it bring you down.
If someone's being mean
All you need to know is
You're no different from them.

If you are racist,
Ask yourself why!

Jessica Weatherley (11)
Gillotts School, Henley-on-Thames

War

People v people, guns v guns
Underground trudges, concentration camps.
People dying and people smiling
Busy streets, gunshots.

People v people, guns v guns
Punishments coming, people ration.
Leaders on trucks, people on ground
Next minute you know, he's down.

People v people, guns v guns
People being hit, people being shot.
Bullets on the ground, blood on the floor
No help, no doctors, no hope.

People v people, guns v guns
Tents, camouflage, guns.
Parades storming, houses blown up
No one can do anything we're all done.

Dylan Rees (12)
Gillotts School, Henley-on-Thames

War

Bang, another gun fires,
Aaahhh, another man screams,
Crash, another bomb falls,
Silence
Another man dead.

The blood drips,
The bomb explodes,
The gun gets loaded,
Another man dead.

The next bomb falls,
The next man screams,
The next bomb lands,
Another man dead.

Emily Townsend (11)
Gillotts School, Henley-on-Thames

Smoking

I don't understand
Smoking's not cool!
It shortens your life,
That's not good at all.

It will make your lungs
Black, disgusting, putrid and rotten.
You will get lung cancer,
Have you forgotten?

Cigarettes are expensive
They don't come cheap.
Cough, cough, cough!
Your lungs are becoming weak.

So, quit smoking now
Before it's too late.
Don't be so stupid
Your future awaits.

Lauren Way (13)
Gillotts School, Henley-on-Thames

Down Goes The Forest!

Crash, burn, sizzle
Down went the forest
All the animals are dead
Up came the shopping centre.

Squish goes the sofa
Brr goes the TV
No one outside
It's a ghost town
Well . . . the X Factor's on.

What would I do without my TV?
I would die without my phone!
Boom goes the planet
What will you say then?

Elizabeth Landen (12)
Gillotts School, Henley-on-Thames

Racist

It's so mean to be racist to any of the races,
Don't make fun of a name because we're all the same.
Doesn't matter if your black, doesn't matter if you're white,
Don't worry about that, it will be alright.

It's so mean to be racist, I don't like it, I hate it,
To do it is bad, it makes people sad.
Doesn't matter if you're black, doesn't matter if you're white,
Don't worry about that, it will be alright.

It's so mean to be racist, don't type it or say it
Don't make fun of a name because the colour of their face.
Doesn't matter if you're black, doesn't matter if you're white,
Don't worry about that, it will be alright.

It's mean to be racist here or other places,
It's not very funny to mock a foreign country.
Doesn't matter if you're black, doesn't matter if you're white,
Don't worry about that, it will be alright.

Calum Hoskins (12)
Gillotts School, Henley-on-Thames

Bullying

To wake up in the morning
To have the focus of going to school
To be the reason of the meaning
Why do they have to be so cruel?

The laughter surrounding you
The tears waiting to fall down your face
Their might only be a few but they make me feel blue
Run away, run away from you!

Bullying hurts
It starts with one word
Stupid, dumb, the words I hear
Well guess what? They are my biggest fear!

Alina Budden (13)
Gillotts School, Henley-on-Thames

A Broken Heart

Feeling his soft fur every day
Made me happy the whole time.
Made me feel like I'm okay
Even though he wasn't mine.

Have you ever felt like there's something missing?
That something needs to be let out.
His perfect furry cheeks made for kissing
That I will always have to live without.

His name was Button, he was my neighbour's rabbit.
One day he disappeared, everyone was sad.
A fox, a cat, a kite? He'd had it.
Things were looking very bad.

Six days past, still no sign
But then he darted past!
He had been hiding the whole time, he was fine
And everyone said, 'At last!'

Lottie Bell (13)
Gillotts School, Henley-on-Thames

Taken Lives

My heart begins to pound
She smiles at me
Looks at the ground
It's hard to see.

She breaks into a run
Hops on the side
Leaps towards the sun
Engulfed by the tide.

I fall to my knees
She took her life
I beg and plead
As I reach for my knife.

Seamus Bringmann (13)
Gillotts School, Henley-on-Thames

War!

Two different countries disagree
A war begins across a sea
The armies meet on great big plains
One known objective in their brains

For centuries Man has fought this way
We're killing our children every day
The supposedly superior human race
Is acting like the animals we are about to erase

All this war is extremely wrong
Every life is precious and not too long
Our world and its creatures are all vey sad
For all this suffering, we humans must be mad

Is there nothing we can do to stop all this war?
Yes, there is, talking, instead of fighting on a moor
The words that we speak are quite powerful things
And ending this war, how much joy that will bring.

Lucy Moran (11)
Gillotts School, Henley-on-Thames

War

His children laugh, his children play
Days go by, day by day.

Father's out once again
Risking his life to pay the price
Writing to Mother again again.

He's a superhero we like to say
Saving the world every day.

His children weep, his children pray
Waiting for that day, that day, that day.
Never again until they reach their time
When they meet each other in paradise.

Beatrice Fox-Wilson (12)
Gillotts School, Henley-on-Thames

Smoking

Brown tobacco burning, smoking me to death.
Unable to run or hide as it drifts into my throat.
An uncontrollable cough burbling too late with sticky mucus,
The lungs already have a coat.

My career is up and running but I can't think without a fag,
If I let my habit go I will become a drag.
My feelings and my friends are restricted
Even my breath and my clothes are addictive.

It seemed fun at the time, at least, while it lasted,
Now my heart and lungs are plastered.
At first it was a joke against the law,
Now it's just an addictive bore.

Another packet rings the change,
Who shall share my dart and stick?
Who will be my friend
When it comes to the end?

Rhys Walker (13)
Gillotts School, Henley-on-Thames

Home

No words, bar bereft
No emotions, bar sadness
Plus a pinch of excitement
That's how I feel.
Step into my shoes
Feel what I feel
As the car drives away
'Tis like my life drifts astray.
Wish I could stop, rewind the clock
I ain't joking
Wish I could wake up in Scotland
And never move away again.

Keir James (13)
Gillotts School, Henley-on-Thames

Just Another Person

Why are people allowed to do this?
People being judged on their appearance
It's the unity and acceptance that I truly miss.
Why is it that people have such hatred in their minds?
For just human beings and all their different kinds.
People today are as shallow as a paddling pool
Others make me feel like a nobody and a fool.
Children ask me why should their parents
Pay taxes for me to go to school?
But I reply with sadness, I'm not breaking any rules.
Surely I shouldn't be judged on the tone of my skin
Maybe people don't realise their actions are such a sin.
The horrific abuse I put up with when I'm visiting a public place
They think that I'm a freak just because of my race.
I'm not so different if you get to know me,
I'm just another person, part of this world,
If you don't look you'll see.

Jordanna Daruvalla-Davies (12)
Gillotts School, Henley-on-Thames

War, Endless War

War, endless war never ever ending,
Everyone's just pretending
That's it's okay
But nobody knows there is no end to this day.

Away saving your life
Leaving alone the mother of two, single wife,
But brother and sister sleep well
Remembering they can live happy without having to dwell.
War, endless war, never ever ending
But now the family's mending
Hoping, believing soon you'll come back our way
So for now we can all cross our fingers and pray.

Carmen Austin-Hawkins (13)
Gillotts School, Henley-on-Thames

WWII

They march in the abyss
With guns at their wrist
When all of a sudden
Boom! With a shudder
They're dead.

Children running
Bombs booming
Houses crumbling
Bodies wasting, wasting away

Ground shaking
People making
Making guns
Why do this?

They do it for land and money our so called *friends.*

Jack Eagle (12)
Gillotts School, Henley-on-Thames

Death

Death is a never-ending force
You never know when it will attack
It will never give up
One second you could be there and then the next
Gone!
You never see it coming
It likes to play with people
Messing with their heads
Tormenting them
Hurting them
Just remember . . .
You're never safe!

Harry Waiton (14)
Gillotts School, Henley-on-Thames

The Endless Fight

Slowly I shy away
The corner is where I stay.
I am like no other,
My heart is pure as gold
But when I am hit, whipped or beat
My true colours begin to show.
They think it doesn't hurt
But inside I'm dying.
No Frisbee is thrown,
Neither stick nor ball.
Whenever I run away they don't seem to call.
It's like I'm not here
Whenever they're near
They just don't seem to care.
They don't treat me right
It's an endless fight
Between dog and man.

Lorna Cousins (13)
Gillotts School, Henley-on-Thames

War

War is hunger and starvation.
War is us as a nation.
War is pointless, it has no meaning.
War causes heartache, loss and bad feeling.

War is victory.
War is gain.
War is history.
War is pain.

War is loved ones that are lost.
Wars are won but at a cost.

War is death.
War is tears.
Wars don't end
They last for years.

Macy Gilmore (11)
Gillotts School, Henley-on-Thames

Cows Vs Sheep

Sheep are woolly though cows are furry.
Sheep are soft though cows are bumpy.
Sheep produce wool though cows produce milk.
Sheep like grass though cows like hay.
Sheep are cute though cows are pretty.
Sheep say 'Baa' though cows say 'Moo!'
Sheep make nice carers though cows make *fudd rucking* good burgers!

Cows have black splodges though sheep can be completely black.
Cows give birth to calves though sheep give birth to lambs.
Cows can give beef jerky though sheep can give lamb chops.
Cows live in fields though sheep live in meadows.
Beef isn't kosher though lamb is.
Male cows are called bulls though male sheep are called rams.
Cows have long tails though sheep have short tails.

Despite their difference we love them both.
It's a shame that they just end up getting eaten or scared in the end.

Syd Harrison Lambert (12)
Gillotts School, Henley-on-Thames

Stereotypes

S tupid because you're blonde
T errorist because you wear a turban
E xotic because you're from the east
R acist because you're white
E xciting because you're daring
O range because you're from Essex
T ough because you have tattoos
Y obbo because you're young and wear a hoodie
P opular because you think highly of yourself
I nteresting because you're clever
N atural and sweet because you wear no make-up
G ay because you're camp and like pink.

Bea Barefield (13)
Gillotts School, Henley-on-Thames

War

People were shouting
People were screaming
All you could hear were cries.

People were frightened
People were scared
All you could feel was fear.

People were shooting
People were dying
All you could see was horror.

People were leaving
All their belongings
All they had was gone.

People were watching
On the news
And all they did was nothing.

Valentina Fragala (11)
Gillotts School, Henley-on-Thames

War!

Bombs are flying
People are dying
Footballers kick a ball
Fighters die and badly fall
Yet they earn more
Footballers let us down every year
But fighters are the reason were still here
I hate war
It should be against the law
It won't solve your problem
But it will just cause more
Be proud of them, love them and be glad we have them!

Brittney Williams (12)
Gillotts School, Henley-on-Thames

An Animal Has No Choice

An animal has no choice.
The chicken will soon be dinner for two;
It will be killed, plucked and made nice and moist.
The sheep will be nothing but a small white rug.
The cow will be a burger served with a cup
Of Coke made from the pig's own fat
And the human will sit there and eat them all up.

An animal has no choice.
If a dog can't sit, high five or dance,
It will be sent to the pound without a second glance.
If a horse can't jump over eight feet
It will be sold or put to sleep.

Neglected and starved,
Unwanted, extinct,
What have they done
To ever deserve this?

Heather Graham (12)
Gillotts School, Henley-on-Thames

Getting Older

G etting worried about the slightest things
R unning away from my pride possession
O n my mind there is pain
W ondering when this will be all over
I will not forget you my love
N ever let go
G etting older is tough

O h how we had so many memories
L oving you each day
D on't forget my saying
E ver yours, mine
R emember me, I will remember you, don't worry darling I love you too.

Tess Hearn (13)
Gillotts School, Henley-on-Thames

The Jungle

Birds are squawking in the treetops,
Feeding and preening until they form flocks.

Tigers roaring non-stop
Devouring prey before it rots.

Bugs and creatures crawling in the undergrowth
Legs, feelers and slime are all so gross.

Trees whistling in high-pitched voices
So many species, too many choices.

Leaves are falling to the jungle floor
Bedding and food, it's the jungle law.

Monkeys swing from branch to branch
If you're lucky enough to get a glance.

Fruit growing all year round
Creatures gathering from trees and ground.

Jack Spiers (12)
Gillotts School, Henley-on-Thames

The Thick Black Smoke

Smoking is a virus
The smoke clogs up inside us
Some call it a blessing others a curse
All I know there's nothing worse
The thick black smoke behind us.

The hungry cloud that hasn't been filled
Enjoying humans to feel its chill
Any more smoke and it'll black out he sun
People still do it even if they know it's not fun
The thick black smoke beside us.

In the past it hasn't said
Now lots of people have wound up dead
Those who died before they shouted
No one knew that smoking could
The thick black smoke in front of us.

Maxim Flynn (12)
Gillotts School, Henley-on-Thames

The Last Days

As I sat there staring at his weak and bloodshot eyes,
I realised that this would be the last chance that I would ever get to see his face.
I still remember staring at his mouth
Every time he took a mouthful
Of the dreaded substance known as a cigarette.
I always overheard the screaming and shouting of them saying,
'You are just paying to kill yourself!'
As he sleeps, his teeth and nails are yellowed with nicotine.
The room is filled with his toxic lungs filling up the air as he breathes in and out.
When the doctor told me that it would be his last days I was speechless.
I looked down onto the floor.
As I stared the tears rolled off my pale destroyed face.
It felt like someone had shot me in the stomach
As I collapsed onto the clean floor of the hospital
I said my goodbyes and watched the machine speak for itself
Beep . . . beep . . . beep . . . beep!

Isobel Peacock (13)
Gillotts School, Henley-on-Thames

War Poem

War means terror all over the world
Dying, crying, fear fills our hearts
Fighting in weathers hot or cold.

Bombed houses leaving families homeless
Soldiers wandering if they will return home
People killing each other as if they were soulless
And devastating battlefields laden with blood and bone.

Massive factories building bombs which go *bang!*
Planes being rested for those willing pilots
And workers working with aching hands!

So how can we stop this terror?

Joseph Neighbour (12)
Gillotts School, Henley-on-Thames

The Racism Poem

Why is there racism, we're all not the same
Just unique in our own different way
There are lots of races on the earth
All born their own way since birth.
Why can people be so mean?
We're all really on the same team
Just fighting a big battle for world peace.
We must work together and treat everyone equally.
Why do you care?
You don't have to stare
Call them horrible names, you know they have feelings in there
Lets all be kind, share our love and live in harmony.

Cameron Jones (12)
Gillotts School, Henley-on-Thames

What War Brings

As I ponder in my ghastly trench,
My mind is focused on my ideal paradise.
The sound of bombs detonating around me makes me weep.
It is the cold tears that snap me back into reality.
'Gas! Gas!' The floor rumbles beneath me,
The gas is as green as grass.
I reach for the picture of my wonderful, wife and children,
The picture is what pushes me forward.
It's the hope of seeing their innocent faces again.
War brings sadness, war brings disaster,
War brings the feeling of missing home.
I will see them again, as long as the gas doesn't catch me!

Samuel Lawrence (13)
Gillotts School, Henley-on-Thames

Poem About War

The sirens sound
As the planes go round and round.
The old church is on fire
And the people call their leader a liar.
There is a loud *thud*
As the soldiers tread through sticky mud.
The father lies dead near a gun
Killed by his own son.
Chaos takes place all around,
Small children are lost then found.
The town is full of hope and glory
But the graves alone will tell the story.

Harry Mackreth (12)
Gillotts School, Henley-on-Thames

Rise Of The Machine

The clanking of machines
What can all this mean?
The inhuman voice of thank you
If the companies win, we lose.

Job applications thrown in the bin,
Every interview taking it on the chin.
Did we know technology would win
The machines have become king.

They don't have a salary
But they need a clean
This is the rise of the machine.

Greg McDonald (13)
Gillotts School, Henley-on-Thames

Put A Stop To Bullying!

Bullying is horrible
Bullying is cruel
Don't ever be a bully as it's very, very cruel.

Behind her tears is anger
Behind her face is fear
That no one really understands
Is where she goes form here.

All they ask for is one friend
That will help them to the end
Laughter and to be jolly is all I need
It's a very, very good friend indeed.

Millie Hargreaves (11)
Gillotts School, Henley-on-Thames

Spectacular Trees

Trees are spectacular, trees, spectacular trees
Blowing in the wind, howling in the breeze,
Trees, trees oh wonderful trees.

They're being cut down, thrown away,
Please help the trees,
It's best that way!

They give us oxygen
They keep us alive
What have they done to deserve this life?
So come on trees, stay alive!

Serena Soroka (12)
Gillotts School, Henley-on-Thames

Stereotyping

I wish it would stop
Wishing I hadn't got
So wrapped up in my thoughts
I couldn't cope with all the taunts
The way they would stop and stare
It was as if they didn't care
They didn't want me there
Just because of the sound of my voice
They laugh at me as if I have a choice.

Charlie Cooper (13)
Gillotts School, Henley-on-Thames

Peaches

The boy in his bed went into his head
Travelled to Greece to get some peace
Away from his noisy family.
His dad was snoring oh so boring.
His mum was singing his ears were ringing.
His brother was whining, whilst his sister was dining.
Oh such a noisy family!
Back in Greece he lay on the beach
Reaching for a big, fat, juicy peach.

George Weait (12)
Gillotts School, Henley-on-Thames

War

War fighting lives being cost.
War families being split up.
War all the lives it costs.
War wish them luck.
War the banging of the guns
War the thumping of their hearts.
War the screaming mums.
War this is how it starts.

Megan Cheney (13)
Gillotts School, Henley-on-Thames

The Poetry Games

The machines are fast at work,
Human faces with a smirk
Nature waits behind the wind
Hiding and hiding but never seen.

Nature strikes without warning
Even though nature is still swarming
The strike causes a natural disaster
And causes a massive palaver.

Humans never learn their lesson
Building machines and never stopping
Even though the rainforest is still cropping
But the humans always have persistence
Keep going and human's fate is creeping into distance.

Nature is an invisible wall
Compared to nature, machines are small
Don't kill the world and don't be sour
Because nature always has more power.

Jake Treasure (13)
Gillotts School, Henley-on-Thames

Underwater Discoveries

Seas, seas beautiful seas from bashful storms to the warming breeze.
Seas hold surprises like underwater prizes
From a brand new fish to an old fish fossil.
Seas, seas beautiful seas
From bashful storms to the warming breeze.
Seas hold many creatures and underwater features
From a coral reef to an underwater leaf.
Seas, seas beautiful seas
From bashful storms to the warming breeze.

Peter Andreou (12)
Gillotts School, Henley-on-Thames

Slender Man

Sitting in my room
All alone
My parents are away
Far from home.

Hide your children
Lock your door
Always beware
The bottom floor.

A tap on the window
A creak on the stair
All I know is
Avoid his glare.

Hide your children
Lock your door
Always beware
The bottom floor.

The click of a lock
I tremble with fear
All I know is
He's very near!

Hide your children
Lock your door
Always beware
The bottom floor.

The whisper of breath
The *thud* of the door
All I know is
For me he hunts for.

Hide your children
Lock your door
Always beware
The bottom floor.

Josh Godwin (11)
Henry Box School, Witney

My Dog

My dog is funny
My dog is sweet
My dog has got
Four furry feet.

His fur is black
His fur is shiny
He is two foot tall
So he is not tiny.

A beautiful face
With big brown eyes
No one would guess
They could ever tell lies.

He has got
A glistening nose
That is cold and wet
As every visitor knows.

My dog is funny
My dog is sweet
My dog has got
Four furry feet.

His tail wags
Non-stop
Of all the dogs
He is the top.

He loves his dad
He loves his mummy
But best of all
He loves his tummy.

Can you guess
What breed he is
Is he a Lab?
Of course he is!

Tatiana Zanre (13)
Henry Box School, Witney

My Five Senses

Such a sight I saw:
The orangey, red sky at sunset
Painting a picture as it hides
Behind the trees with the moon bringing
In the dusk.

Such a sight I saw.

Such a sound I heard:
The soft gentle rain tapping on the window
Asking me to come out
They were swinging about
As the wind pushing them back and forth.

Such a sound I heard.

Such a taste I tasted:
The warm thickness of chocolate
As it dribbles down my chin
Making me think of Mr Cadbury's
Chocolate heaven.

Such a taste I tasted.

Such a smell I smelt:
The warm smell of chocolate cake
As it fills me with joy and looks at me
As if it wants me to eat it.

Such a smell I smelt.

Such a feeling I felt:
The feeling of my dog's warm head
As it fills me with sadness
And how much I miss him now he is gone
Such a feeling I felt.

Daniel Wastie (11)
Henry Box School, Witney

A Mother's Work Is Never Done

A mother's work is never done
While fathers sit around upon their bum
A mother cooks and cleans and nags
Never noticing the sags

Upon her haggard and tired face
Too busy tying up a shoelace
For her lazy and gluttonous child
It's a miracle her language is always mild!

And she's always saying 'Eat your carrots and peas
Won't you do it for Mummy, please?'
Also she's never allowed to sit down
Or have fun and lounge around.

Her rusty old pathetic car
Hasn't been to a good health spa
For about a decade or so
Too busy fighting her kitchen foe

Which are grease and germs,
But also looking after, on half terms,
Her vile and disgusting child
And her husband who's since gone wild.

However, one day,
In a bright and sparkling May
She said, 'Why am I doing all this
Is there something I have missed?'

Well that's it; I'm not doing it anymore!'
And she dumped the clothes she was holding onto the floor
And no one has ever seen this mother since
Perhaps she's found her handsome prince!

Laurie Day (12)
Henry Box School, Witney

Willow

Look at the fields in flower
All turned into bloom
In the black bog behind us
Stands a willow covered in shroom.

The crying tree begs us
Set me free again
The bogs firm grip holds it
Like a prisoner wrapped in chains.

The arms that droop and swing around
Are as placid as can be
The bog grabs its helpless children
As they start to plea.

The children start to cry again
The frost is far too near
The once bright little children
Droop and fill with fear.

The shields upon its branches
Shrivel up and rust
Travelling in the wind
They crumble into dust.

The willow's anger starts to grow
All its possessions are lost
The bog refreezes over
Its actions have cost.

Willow is dusted with white powder
Its skin begins to fall
Now it's frosted over
All that's left to do is bawl.

Charlie Dunstan (14)
Henry Box School, Witney

Vampire Smile

It's lonely being a vampire
Not having a single friend
No one wants to talk to me
Just evil thoughts they send.

As I clean up all of the rooms
I try my best to be calm
It's so hard when the children walk in
I just want to plunge my fangs into their arm.

When they finally look at me
I give a friendly bright grin
They scream and rush out of the room
Being a vampire is the greatest sin.

My childhood was a disaster
When I went to Vampire High
The others threw weapons at me
They almost made me cry.

In the human world I am locked up
Slayers try to kill me
They slash at my throat
To get out I need a key.

I am kept as a prisoner every day
I long to breath fresh air
As everybody runs from me
I hope somebody will see I care.

All I long for in life is a friend
Someone who will smile
I guess I should give up
I will keep waiting for a while.

Kiera Rhodes (13)
Henry Box School, Witney

Belsen

I knew her name and that was all,
Except that she was all alone.
She sat curled up upon a stair
Her shadow a depressing clone.

She seemed so strange, I wondered why
She simply sat and wept all day.
She ignored all who spoke to her
And never had a thing to say.

She wore a star upon her chest
And that meant that she was a Jew.
Even if I wanted to be her friend
There was nothing at all that I could do.

Apparently she was not like me
And that meant I could not go near.
I couldn't even comfort her
Or wipe her tears or calm her fear.

Then suddenly she disappeared
Behind a crowd of soldier men.
I heard her cries, I felt her pain
But I left her trapped inside her pen.

I knew I couldn't help her though
For she was her and I was me.
I told my mother of their mistake
And she just said it was to be.

Then she was thrown into a truck
She begged for me to save her soul.
The little girl was dragged away
As her life ends no bell will toll.

Eden Southey (13)
Henry Box School, Witney

Snow White

Blood red were her lips
Snow white was her skin
With her emerald eyes
And raven black hair
It leaves no doubt
Who is the fairest of them all.

Coal black were her lips
Old and wrinkly was her skin
With her jade green eyes
And ice blonde hair
It leaves no doubt
Who wants dearest Snow White's
Innocent heart.

'Mirror mirror
On the wall
Who is the fairest
Of them all?'
Was the witch's cry.
'Snow White'
Was the mirror's reply
Then tonight she will die!
The witch declared.

Blood red were her lips
Snow white was her skin
Blood red was the poisonous apple
With a bite on its side
That fell out of Snow White's
Dead, cold hand.

Emma Roberts (14)
Henry Box School, Witney

The Diary Of Courage

A girl writes a diary in a country miles away
Of something so simple to me
A girl takes courage to follow her dreams of an education
Something to me that is free
Free from fear and violence, this is something she expresses in her diary.

This diary is set at school in Pakistan
And all the girl wants is to learn
Although 'Girls cannot go,' say the Taliban
But it's courage you have to earn.

The girl goes to school walking down danger's path
And all who know life could end
Although this girl is very brave and very smart
Swat valley is not a place you can mend.

But on one normal afternoon at the end of the day
'Girls should go to school,' she said
The Taliban follow her and make the girl pay
By putting the gun to her head.

The bullets are fired,
Bang! Bang! Bang!
Surely by now she is dead
She has survived and will stay alive
But now she is getting better in bed.

Now think of your life
Are you in danger
Will you be stopped to follow your dreams?
The answer to that is you're not in strife
The girl, Malala Yousafzai is as right as it seems.

Macy Netysy (12)
Henry Box School, Witney

A Winter Night

Softly padding her cloven hooves into the icy cold snow,
Wobbles around a newborn fawn with her mother the strong muscled doe.
Learning what these cold white flakes are,
Hopping around but she can't go far.

Nearby sits a hungry wolf searching for his dinner,
He sees a rabbit through the white trees, catches, he's a winner.

Beyond the trees a herd of reindeer
Their heads heavy with antler headgear.
Tapping their hooves through the rock solid ice
Searching for crumbs of something nice.

The sleepy bear rests in his room
As snow falls outside in the gloom.
No clue of the white blanket that thickens outside,
He just stays where he is well supplied.

Red like blood in the white lurks the bandit fox
Snatching rabbits, their peace he shocks.
He takes them back to his tree trunk den
Eats them then sneaks off once again.

Masked raccoons walk tightrope branches
Causing tree fall avalanches.
Steal any food they can find
Whatever there is they do not mind.

Creatures of the snow galore
Howl, squeal, squeak and roar.
As the moon and stars supervise the night
Like a large shiny spotlight.

Nelle Hardy (13)
Henry Box School, Witney

When I First Met You

When I saw you it was love at first sight
These through the dull and fatuous light
I saw you come near and smile
It was the biggest smile I saw in a while.
You blushed a deep red as a giggle showed.

I asked you your name; it took awhile for you to say
You apologised, I shrugged and said 'That's okay.'
I touched your arm as you shivered
The wind floated by when the trees quivered
You softly whispered, 'I really like you.'

I touched your hand, it was cold as ice
I asked you to hang out. You said, 'Nice.'
Before you went you kissed me
You went inside, swaying trees I could see
Looking at me with intimidating looks.

As I strolled down the road I sigh
As the rain fell from the high.
I saw you again by my side
I left the embarrassment inside hide.
My arm wrapped round your shoulders.

You clutched my hand and dragged me
The rain made it hard for me to see.
Back to your house we walked
The wind howled as he stalked
Me and the girl who I just met.

Ben Costley (14)
Henry Box School, Witney

When You Left Me All Alone

When you left me all alone
I was sad, nowhere to go.

I searched for you, I prayed
For you I cannot trade.
I found your body, cold and dead
Your soul up there, above my head.

When you left me all alone
I was sad, nowhere to go.

When you looked on me, over here
I'd lift my head up and peer.
My heart tears and is ripped out
Tears fill my eyes, I start to pout.

When you left me all alone
I was sad, nowhere to go.

But I made a choice to meet you
I will come there to greet you.
So right now I am here
But I'm on my way, don't fear.

When you left me all alone
I was sad, nowhere to go.

I'm right here, we're together
I'm happy right now and forever.

Dan Weston (12)
Henry Box School, Witney

Some Days

(Inspired by David Harmer's 'Some Days')

Henry Box is a silky spider's web grabbing us in
Struggling to get out, we are epically failing.
On days like this I feel it's a disaster
6 hours and 5 minutes of horrible torture.
Other days, this school is like an aeroplane soaring through the sky.
Every year we'll see older children leave and we will say goodbye.

Ethan Barrett (11)
Henry Box School, Witney

The Bullies

They held me up,
Watched me bleed,
Smiled together,
Laughed at me,
Kicked me up,
Broke me down
And on all their faces
They wore a frown.
They chanted names,
They hit my head.
I fell unconscious
And then they fled.
The pain still stays,
The days pass by.
I question my life,
I want to die.
But life gets better
I promise you.
Be yourself,
Be fully true.
Tell a teacher,
Report the names.
You'll be happy,
Bullying is not a game.

Aoife Burnett (13)
Henry Box School, Witney

The Man In The Snow

The man could spend 20 years in the snow.
He's standing right there but to him you don't know.
He can see you but he sees right through
The past and the cold and everything new.
You ignore him on purpose so how is this news?
You set your own life but please try to choose.
So when you next see him, give him a hello
Because the man you don't know could spend 20 years in the snow.

Finn Miles-Collett (13)
Henry Box School, Witney

Homage To Christianity

Hallelujah! Praise the Lord!
Shh . . . Dad, what's the score?

The world really is a changing place
With no more stereotypes of sex, religion or race.
People all standing hand in hand,
Respecting all borders, sharing all land.
Ha ha, if only this was truly the case!

Spread the Gospel! Let it be!
Shh . . . Mum, what's for tea?

Man shall lie in bed with other men
Without prejudices, from others, amen!
Woman shall speak in church,
She shall be heard, she shan't just perch
Ha ha, if it's not now, then please, tell me when?

Glory to God! Our true King!
Shh . . . Kids, what's that ring?

The world really is a changing place
Equality is rife, those different showing face.
No war, no crime, no hunger nor thirst.
None of us punished with the Sin of the first.
Ha ha, of course, this is never to be the case!

Bethany Murphy (17)
Henry Box School, Witney

The Hunger Games

(Inspired by 'The Hunger Games' by Suzanne Collins)

Such a fantastic flavour
May the odds be ever in your favour
So much loving blood
So much to make a flood
For those of you who lose
Only death can choose
The winner will be showered in fame
Happy hunger games.

Ben Warner (12)
Henry Box School, Witney

World Peace

Swing! Smack! That's all you hear
I can see dead bodies far and near
Through light and darkness, sweat and tear
It's a really bad place out here.

It's cold and dark, I can't see
But a hero, I must be
Out here you don't make friends
Cos it leads to heartbreak in the end.

Lots of tactics we are told to do
But between me and you
If a gunshot is fired all hell breaks loose
My code name out there is 'Goose'

Three months I've been here
I used to have a normal career
But this is for me, I will achieve
World peace you better believe!

The war has stopped and it's due to me
But unfortunately my death has come
So they planted me a tree
Engraved for me.

Kai Rapley (13)
Henry Box School, Witney

The Bully

The school bully thinks he's tough.
He likes to scare and all things rough.
He stomps round by the playground wall,
trying to make people fall.
The victim is very upset, these things can also happen on the net.
Everyone's scared, so they join in,
trying to make the victim feel grim.
The teacher must be told, so these things can be resolved.
The bully said he won't do it again,
now the victim is no longer in pain.

Grace Iszkula (11)
Henry Box School, Witney

The War

Why do soldiers have to fight,
Can't we just be friends?
In rain and thunder they hang on tight
But why do they die?

What happens when you die?
I desperately need to know.
Do you fly away for a year and a day
Or do you just live in the clouds?

The war, the war, why do we have war?
Tanks, guns, bullets
And grenades.
Why do they have to die?

I wish war could stop
So none of the soldiers drop.
Poppies will grow to remember them all
But why, oh why do they have to die?

The soldiers are brave
But some are scared
If only they didn't
Have to go.

Georgina Hammond (11)
Henry Box School, Witney

The Dragon

English dragon in all its might
Gave to the dark the gift of light
With power it roars
Flexing its perfect claws
In the air it hangs
The moon on its perfect fangs
To royalty it hails
A beauty with scales.

Amy Edwards (12)
Henry Box School, Witney

Destiny Diamond

Destiny Diamond lives in a field
She comes to school with her lips unsealed
Bleating out the worst of words
She likes to poke dead birds.

Her hair is as wild as a chimpanzee
She comes to school smelling like tea
Her skin's as pink as kitten's nose
I think she needs to get a hose.

Her dress is as ragged as a ripped autumn leaf
Don't even get me started on her teeth!
Her eyes are as wide as a frog's fly hole
You wouldn't want to meet her she's a troll.

She reminds me of a cannibal goat
I think she needs to get a coat.
She's as skinny as a rake
Stay away from her for your own sake.

So Destiny Diamond needs a life
But be careful she carries a knife
I need to go before she comes
Or she'll beat me with her big fat thumbs!

Alyssa Nurden (12)
Henry Box School, Witney

Midnight Chocs

You can't resist them
One bite like a crystal gem
Creamy milk chocs and bitter dark
Leaving a chocolate mark
Sitting and taking one bite
So right
The deal is done
What fun!

Amelia Robinson (12)
Henry Box School, Witney

Meaning Of Life

Every person is different,
And being different is what they fear.
Fear is the sign of failure
Failure is drawing near.

Life is a big book,
Book containing secrets and hopes.
Hopes craft your future,
Future is full of scopes.

Life is what happens while you are busy making other plans,
Plans are nothing, planning is everything.
Everything has beauty but not everyone sees it,
It can give you a trance.

Every man has the right to decide his own destiny,
Destiny is no matter of chance; it is a matter of choice.
Choice is when you have too many selections,
Selections sometimes bring out your inner voice.

Atmosphere and the environment shape you,
You are the keeper of your fate.
Fate doesn't deal the right cards that doesn't mean you should stop.
Stop only when you life comes to an end and don't let others make you hate.

Divya Varghese (13)
Henry Box School, Witney

Soul

The eldest of sons
Each day you grow older
Each moment I'm watching your soul slowly wither
The right for your body
The flesh of your soul
Will die through the years
Your body he stole!

Brontë Moulder (12)
Henry Box School, Witney

Through The Eyes Of The Outsider

I see the world in black and white with maths and equations,
I see your face when you talk to me, but not your emotions.
Conversations are like a one-way mirror to me, you can see in but I can't,
But that's just how life is for me and I've never known any different.

You see what I think when you talk to me, you know me inside out.
My eyes, my mouth, you decipher for me, the code that you can break.
You think your life's much better than mine, that's what you've got wrong
But that's just how life is for you and you've never known any different.

You say it's only worth living when life's full of emotion and colour,
Red, green, yellow and blue, all colours that mean emotions.
You see people's faces and match the colours trying to know them more,
And that's how you like to live your life, but it's not the same for me.

Life may not be equations for you but that's how I like to see it,
You ask me if life's hard to live, the way that I have to live it.
But after a while I hope you'll learn and start to finally understand,
We're not so different you and I; I've just got a label.

Esther Jackson (13)
Henry Box School, Witney

Memories

So many things have changed
The days have passed and I've grown
Looking back, those sweet and silvery memories.

I remember as a mischievous girl grew
Looking and looking only at the future
She was in a deep trance of the future that she forgot the present
Her grin, her smile, her tears
Can't believe that once she was me.

I remember as the days passed so many deaths but so many lives
I watched as the flowers died and grew, a gentle smile for anew.

Live loving the present, at times live with memories,
Live dreaming for the future but don't abandon the present.

Jiya Thomas (11)
Henry Box School, Witney

Some Days

(Inspired by David Harmer's 'Some Days')

Some days Henry Box is a spider's web trapping charming children
Ensnaring us like a fly
Making us wish we would all die
So horrible it's forcing us to cry.

On those days I wish I was back at home
Eating my mum's freshly baked scone
Wanting to read my favourite poem
Sitting in my room all alone.

Other days school is so much fun!
Teachers amusing us, pun after pun
Hoping the day would never be done
Lessons sending us the whole way to the sun!

On those days I wish it would happen again
I feel there is no one around me but free men
I wish time would stop so I could stay there
There and then.

Nick Wilson (11)
Henry Box School, Witney

The Big Match

He arrives at the ground with the wind in his face,
Defenders scared of his blistering pace.
The team talk starts and the nerves sink in
Nail biting stuff, wondering who's gonna win.
The teams run out to cheers and applause
10 minutes gone, still level scores.
Who has the passion to steal the deal?
Players' hearts pounding, could this be real?
A last minute cross into the box
He strikes a volley with a power of an ox.
The ball hits the net with venom and violence
Goal, goal, goal!
The crowed are silenced.

Elliott Heritage (13)
Henry Box School, Witney

The Best Dog I've Ever Had

I have a cocker spaniel
He is short, fat, black and white.
He may look a bit angry
But he would never ever bite.
He follows me around wherever I go
The only problem is, he is too slow.
He sleeps all day
Plays at night.
My cocker spaniel loves me
He would never run away
He loves to lie on plastic base
On the kitchen floor
At night I can hardly sleep
All he does is snore!
Some people love him
Some people think he's cute.
I think my cocker spaniel Dylan
Is the best dog I've ever had.

Frankie O'Neil (12)
Henry Box School, Witney

Highwayman Of The Night

There he came, on his horse, bandana masking his face,
Trying to get to the carriage, he was keeping up a good pace.
Alongside the carriage he was galloping, on his sturdy black horse,
The carriage he was chasing came to a stop with great force.
He came up to the window, he held out his hand.
They refused to give him their money
So he took out his gun,
Shot the nearest man.
He then got the money
Just like he had planned.
His horse reared up
He held up his gun with might
Then he went,
A highwayman of the night.

Kaylin Boehm (13)
Henry Box School, Witney

The Outsider

He walked into the house
Lonely as a fly,
Shivering from the cold
Winter night's air.

He said nothing as he shuffled
Into the warm
But a muffled 'Thank you'
From behind his old woollen scarf.

He stayed silent throughout his stay
As we gave him food and shelter
He seemed as distant and different
As the sun to the moon.

As he left our home
He seemed a little more lively
But even so, he still departed
As an outsider.

Billy Monahan (13)
Henry Box School, Witney

The Crash On The Marsh

I could hear them drowning
The fog in front of me creeping
The young child crying
The marsh engulfing.

The poor child screaming
I started panicking
The fog became choking
I started running.

The sound became piercing
My eyes started filling
My mouth started trembling
My heart started longing.

Hazel Bicker (15)
Henry Box School, Witney

Some Days

(Inspired by David Harmer's 'Some Days')

Some days this school is a big tidal wave
Ready to sweep you away.
A mass of children swaying with the tide
From lesson to lesson.
On those days I feel like a little fish out of my depth
Hardly daring to breathe.
On other days I feel like a light fluffy cloud
The small mass of water taken from the sea
Controlled by the wind
Each child drifting elegantly
This way and that.
On those days I feel
Like a major contributor
A part of one big thing.

Demelza Cornish (12)
Henry Box School, Witney

Pearls Of The Night

The moon shatters the rolling sea into silver shards
Casting its ancient light across oceans
Shining endlessly into darkness.

Pearls of the night
Reflecting in the sailors eye
Until the dawn is nigh
The pearls sing tonight.

Galaxies, far off in the gloom shimmer
Revealing their metallic fish scales
Dancing behind the night clouds.

Pearls of the night
Reflecting in the sailor's eye
Until the dawn is nigh
The pearls sing tonight.

Rebecca Isherwood-Halliwell (12)
Henry Box School, Witney

Understand

Sometimes they call him simple
Sometimes they call him plain.
But I call him what he is
A boy who doesn't understand.

He doesn't understand emotion
He might not get jokes
But he is what he is
A boy who doesn't understand.

They even call him stupid
And they sometimes call him weird.
But I call him what he is
A boy who doesn't understand.

He might lose his temper
He doesn't like to be touched
But he is what he is
The boy who doesn't understand.

Annie McLean (13)
Henry Box School, Witney

Lost In The Snow!

Lost in the snow
Nobody knows
Shall I shout for help?
How do I get out?

It's cold and crunchy
Falling from the sky
Lands on your nose
And builds up very high.

Put it together
And roll it on the ground
Make a snowman
And make him nice and round.

Lost in the snow
Nobody knows
Shall I shout for help?
How can I get out?

Jessica Bevan (11)
Henry Box School, Witney

Role Models

What are role models?
Well, they aren't what they used to be.
We need to look up to people who make positive changes
Not just the ones that design fashion ranges.

Whatever happened to aspiration?
Why don't people aspire to being an astronaut or prime minister?
People should aim for exciting lives
Not just want to be footballer's wives.

Shouldn't young people discover what's happening in the real world?
Not the airbrushed one?
Nowadays, people read magazines instead of books
It's no longer knowledge that counts, just looks.

Young faces covered in make up
Boob jobs, Botox, short skirts, tight tops
Celebrities 'red carpet ready'
When they walk out the door
It's just not interesting anymore!

Good grades, if you've got them, you're a 'nerd' not a 'popular'
Role models should be people that work hard
At their job or school
Life's not just about being cool.

Let's have better role models and different goals
Let's think about education, environment, economy
Not just the life of a celebrity!

Alessia Grant (12)
Lord Williams's School, Thame

Homeless

Click clack horses trot past
Stamp, stomp people glance and ignore
Shivering in the cold
Wishing you weren't poor.

Staring at your cracked hands
With hardly any food
You sigh with depression
In a very bad mood.

Watching the world go by
Sitting in the damp
Hearing babies cry
Setting up the camp.

Hanging up your clothes
In the winter weather
You look over to a lady's bag
That's been made with precious leather.

You spot across the street
A person being sold
Shaking your head in disgust
You wept in the cold.

In the cold winter nights
You gradually fall asleep
Snoring like a lion
The sound of a car horn wakes you up, *beep!*

Charlotte Brentnall (11)
Lord Williams's School, Thame

The Friends We Have

Friends, they will do anything for you,
Aren't they like sisters who you can trust?
They're the people who are with us whatever we do.

Friends, they are people you can rely on,
They always make you laugh,
You always know they're there even if they're gone.

Friends, you know that they will never laugh at you,
In your heart you will always love them,
And you always know that they love you too.

Friends, they're the people you can do anything with,
From shopping to sleepovers, from talking to karaoke,
You know that friends will be there for however long we live.

Friends, they're like books,
You don't always need them but they're there when we do,
Most of them also make good cooks.

Friends, they entertain us, calm us, excite us,
They are there for fun or for serious,
You know that you can always sit next to them on the bus.

Friends, when you're broken hearted they're always there,
They make our memories and write our future,
You always know in your heart that they care.

Emilie Felicien (11)
Lord Williams's School, Thame

Forever Horses

As carrier bags crisp packets, Coke cans and more
Blow through the street from door to door
Making their way to horse fields nearby
As they eat them up and nearly die.

Calling for help he drops to the floor
His friends join in but everyone ignores
Nobody comes will anyone ever
Will this be the end for horses forever?

Kiera Green (11)
Lord Williams's School, Thame

War

Plane
Why do people have war?
It should be against the law.
We should be calm,
Not armed.

Drop
We should not shoot,
We should not use bombs that pollute.
We should not have to cry
And certainly should not have to die.

Whistle
Building weapons wastes time
And it should be a crime.
Food is under ration
Camouflaged soldiers can't have a sense of fashion.

Bang
The nuclear bomb is falling down to earth
It will destroy a lot more than Perth.
The ugly black piece of rusty metal
Will make a country as weak as a petal.

Death.

Pat Morley (11)
Lord Williams's School, Thame

Weather Change

As the rain comes hurtling down like bombs crashing
The rain bounces off the roofs like machine guns rattling
The sun breaks out and the atmosphere changes
The ground dries out and the water evaporates.
Next comes the snow, oh no!
The ground rumbling like it's angry with the world
People freezing because of the cold.

George Hewitt (11)
Lord Williams's School, Thame

The World Falls . . . Silent

The noise of technology
Crammed to one world
Spread round the Earth
Faster than the words

The noise of networks
Sharing, chatting, harming
Far and still talking
All on one web.

But when that time is over
When the world falls
Into the silence
The silence of Earth.

Planes fall out of the sky
Cars stop the road still
People can't connect
But with the paper and pen

They talk face to face
Back to the normal of
The 100 years ago words
Back to the noise
The noise of the voice.

Alfie Richards (12)
Lord Williams's School, Thame

Polar Bears

Polar bears are as
White as the snow
And in the winter the wind
Begins to blow.

These poor bears
Losing their ice
Global warming
Is not very nice.

We can help these poor
Bears, we can help
Them through this with
The light of our flares.

We can win this
Battle, even if it
Is a pant-load of
Baffle.

We are losing
These things so cute and cuddly
Because we are at home all
Warm and snuggly.

Griff Eden-Parish (11)
Lord Williams's School, Thame

A Broken World

The battlefield's empty
The grass is bloody and dead.
The soldiers lower their weary heads
Just waiting for 'It's over!' to be said.

Many have fallen to the ground
Some are still brawling.
Even though the war is all around
Soldiers are down and crawling.

Most had been shot and were dying
Their bodies were broken and bent.
As they lay sleeping already
The souls are ready to be sent.

The wounded cannot feel the pain
So much they are unable to speak.
Their bodies exhausted and drained
The muscles relax and everything is weak.

The soldiers are waiting for peace
Their bodies in pain from the lead.
Are waiting for their release
Asking themselves am I alive or dead?

Joshua Helgesen-Cross (11)
Lord Williams's School, Thame

Freedom

All I want is freedom,
Freedom to be me.
Is it too much to ask
To forget about my past?

To be me,
All I want to be is free.
Not to be judged
But to have my opinion and not be budged.

My dreams should be given the chance to materialise
Then perhaps people will realise.
I should think my own thoughts
And my life not be so fraught.

My skin colour or faith
Should not act as bait
To allow people to sneer
And say nasty things for me to hear.

I know one day
Everyone will have the chance to say
I have stuck to my guns
And my new life has begun.

Harriet Burdett (12)
Lord Williams's School, Thame

Prices

Money!
Money!
Money!
Everything now costs money!

Forget more for less,
It's more like less for more,
It's getting even worse for people who are poor.

Go to the shop
Looking for some bread,
You'd be lucky
If I'd pay that on my death bed.

Fuel prices
Are rising up,
At that price
I'll run my car on ketchup.

Money!
Money!
Money!
Everything costs money.

Jamie Wiles (11)
Lord Williams's School, Thame

Computer Games

As the humans grow old
Everyone is told about the one virus that infects the Earth
It is the computer games birth.

Kids are good at lazing around
The only thing they hear is a shooting sound
Beating or should I say game
To be fair it is quite lame.

Dad comes in saying, 'Time to do your homework'
But the son just keeps on playing
One hour later all the same
If he keeps on playing he will get eyestrain.

Later on still he is playing the game
But when he hears a new one has come out it is all the same
'Mum, Mum, can I please have that game?'
However she says, 'Stick to the one you got or it won't be the same.'

Computer game cost lots and lots however the manager plots
To get a game everyone will like
A better game than riding your own bike.

Jamie Pytlasinski (12)
Lord Williams's School, Thame

Get Rid Of Racism On The Football Field

Noises here, noises there,
People shouting everywhere
Hurting me with their voice
Saying things that are mean to me.

Paper here, paper there,
Papers thrown everywhere
Showing me things that shouldn't be seen
Waving lots of different banners at me.

Ignorance here, ignorance there
Ignorant people everywhere.
As I step up to take the kick
They all start to boo and hiss.

White people here, black people there,
They treat us all a bit unfair.
Multicultural is the way
For a better place to live and stay!

Harrison Berrell (11)
Lord Williams's School, Thame

Rugby

Mud here, mud there,
Rugby players everywhere.
Snap! Crackle! Pop! There goes a bone
Ring! Ring! There goes the ambulance phone.

No matter what the weather
As long as we all play together.
It's how you play the game
Not seeking any fame.

I love being part of the team
So let's not let off any steam.
I know we play with a funny shaped ball
So let's try and catch it shall we all.

Charlie Jacob Gardiner (11)
Lord Williams's School, Thame

The Times Of Year

When the sun is shining
There's a glow in your heart.
But when it comes to winter
There's only darkness to be touched.

When all the lambs are producing
And blossom is starting to grow.
Then suddenly all the leaves are falling off the trees
And all the lambs have grown.

The wind ruins my soft straight hair
As it brushes through the trees.
Then the rain comes and makes it even worst
Then comes the snow and makes the wind blow.

Hail is hard and sharp and it prickles when it hits me,
I try and dodge it but there's just too much.
Lightning is scary it dashes down from the sky
Thunder isn't that good either.

Mia Jones (11)
Lord Williams's School, Thame

Friendship

Friends will always be there for you
Friends are like a book
Friends will always support you
They are only a phone call away
Without friends you'll be lonely
With friends you won't be lonely
Without friends no one to talk to
With friends someone to talk to
Friendship you will have ups and downs
But you forgive them
That's called trust
Trust you need in a friendship
It doesn't matter if you have a best mate who is a boy
Because that means you're really close to them
Friendship is about caring and trusting in your friend.

Nicole Breed (11)
Lord Williams's School, Thame

Animals

The battle is not yet over
For what every tree is worth
We've killed hundreds of leopards around us
In which the rest are dying on Earth.

You hear the call of a panda
Shouting with its might
What have they done to hurt us?
Why we have damaged the black and white.

The jungles are passing away
And the tigers have all been cleared
Can we change our actions to animals?
So hurry before they've disappeared.

Before the battle is over
And all the animals have gone
Help save the forests and jungles
So please hurry it won't be long.

Isabel Dhanjal (11)
Lord Williams's School, Thame

World War

The men march forwards towards the front line
All of them knowing that they are not returning home again!

Bang! The last gun fires.
The last man falls to the ground
As the bullet enters his flesh.

The world screams for hope
Now there is no hope left.
Widows crying as they have just found out
That their husbands are never returning home again.
All of the bullets have been fired
Fog and smoke now fill the land
Silence creeps in slowly
Smothering the dead.
Families thinking is Dad ever coming back?

William James Chadwick (11)
Lord Williams's School, Thame

The Animals Are Dying

The polar bears are dying out,
The ice caps are melting away.
Why has this started happening?
We have to stop it today!

The orang-utans are dying out
The trees are being taken away.
Why has this started happening?
We have to stop it today!

The tigers are dying out,
The rainforest is being taken away.
Why has this started happening?
We have to stop it today!

All the creatures are dying out,
The habitats are being taken away.
Soon there won't be any animals,
Why does it have to end this way?

Jodie Farrell (11)
Lord Williams's School, Thame

Save The Animals

Animals are dying out
So save them please now.
Their homes are being ruined
Because we're cutting the trees down.

Their fur is being turned into coats
So please stop killing goats.

Crocodile skin is being made into something too!
Handbags, coats even a pair of nice shoes.

If you have a nice rug on your living room floor
It maybe the fur of a lion or the skin of a boar.

Animals are dying out
So save them please now!

Charlotte Freeland (12)
Lord Williams's School, Thame

Friendship

Friendship has its ups and downs
When down it can be the worst time ever
When up it knows no bounds
It's something you want to let go of, never.

Friends don't need to be clever or smart
It's their personality inside
If they have a strong kind heart
Then they will never run away and hide.

Sometimes we take them for granted
But mostly they will be forgiving
Because the seeds of friendship have been planted
And they make life worth living.

A friend is there come rain or shine
They support you when you are troubled
Having a friend feels mighty fine
My happiness is doubled.

Eleanor Brown (11)
Lord Williams's School, Thame

A Paradox Of Trees

Why are trees so hard,
But can be made into card?
And the making of paper
Can be a terrible caper.

When trees are chopped to their maximum
There can be a huge pandemonium.
Wood can be used for burning
And also a tool for learning.

Yet trees can be used for building
You might not realise it is killing
So if you don't hurt the trees
Many people you will please.

Josiah Andrews (11)
Lord Williams's School, Thame

Feeling Peckish?

When has a sheep
Gone up to you
Taken your child
And eaten them too?

Screaming lambs
Wanting Mum
Being slaughtered
Not much fun.

What have they ever
Done to you
To make you use them
As your food?

Lamb chops
On the barbecue
Imagine being
Next in the queue.

Jem Mentesh (11)
Lord Williams's School, Thame

This Is War Or Peace

This is how it could be with people loving and caring
Cheeky children chatting away, cheering people to be daring
Not lurking in the shadows, not hiding themselves away
Coming out enjoying the love, the joy of every day.

This is madness, craziness, killing of all joy
I mean men going into battle when they are actually just a boy
People screaming, questioning all of the humanity
Begging boisterous rulers to stop all of their insanity.

Is this a poem of siblings fighting
Or is it a poem of disparity?
Is this because of inciting
Or is it just plain barbarity?

No, this is all of them rolled into one
If only there could be none
No, this is something much much more
This is hate, this is love, this is war.

Rebecca Huglin (11)
Lord Williams's School, Thame

Fruit And Veggies Are Good

Green
Gorgeous green peppers are so yummy
Brussels sprouts are so scrummy
Peas and beans are in my tummy.

Red
Ruby red peppers taste so great
Tomatoes, eight I ate
Chillies, just as good as a date.

Yellow
Yummy yellow peppers are delicious
Lemons aren't that pernicious
Bananas are very nutritious.

Orange
Organic orange peppers, munch, munch, munch
Carrots give a super crunch
Mangoes going in my lunch.

Emily Baillie (11)
Lord Williams's School, Thame

Education Is The Key To Success

Education is the key to the closed door of success
It enables you to reach success
When you think all doors are closed
And when you believe you can't be successful in life
If you have education as your first priority
You can assure yourself that you have the power to succeed
And your dreams come through.

When you have education it helps dreams come through for your future
And when you think all hope is lost
You've got one hope left on you
If you have education
Education is free and compulsory for you
If you are ready to succeed.

Education is the famous thing required
Without it, it defeats you and your future success
Education is when you learn and gain something
For your freedom to success
Education is important right from infant
The future of a person can be unpredictable
If you lack education
Education is a life sustaining material
Education empowers a person to become a leader
There is nothing quite like education
Development, growth or new invention.

For any country or nation
Its essential to get a good education
Don't allow anyone to take your dream away from you
'Cause you can be greater than the greatest
And nothing can ever defeat you from success
And also make sure no one distracts you away from education.

Life is difficult without education
It makes your life hard to live
And without education it creates a mess
If you don't allow yourself to grow into education
Success will be hard for you to have.

Education offers the opportunity for a person
Education is essential to make a pleasant

And stable living out of a simple quotidian life
Make yourself useful towards your education
Never leave your success at stake.

Success is right near you
Grab it now!
When you have education you can be successful
The key to success is education
Up! Education
Up! Success.

Olayinka Olasehinde (14)
North Oxfordshire Academy, Banbury

Monsters Under The Bed

The monsters are out from under the bed
Prowling the forests, free from your head
Innocence cringes on the fringes
And chivalry is dead
Led by the nose we take pride in our anger
Distracted by pictures feeding our hunger
To hunt them down, run out of town
Willing to believe what is said
Honing fear into a weapon
A pack of wolves we set upon them
We listen to fools, make up our own rules
Until the need is fed
The torches are lit, the pitchforks are raised
We bang on our chests and anger is praised
Whipped into a frenzy we march on the enemy
The only colour seen is red
Sadly it makes us feel better
Absorbing it all right to the letter
A twisted distraction from lack of satisfaction
Let the others think instead
When one is gone we create another
Empathy we need to smother
Mental dealings to avoid the feelings
A sharp stick for the monster under the bed.

Eliza Worden (14)
North Oxfordshire Academy, Banbury

Sob

The killer whale hated, feared
By adults and children alike,
Hatred upon the one so big, so clever
Fear upon the one so skilled a killer.
Sad is it that the big black fish
Threatened, endangered, will cease to exist.
In years to come not a soul will know
Of the big black fish
That swam the oceans from right to left.

'Save the orca,' people cry
As if that fear in them has died.
The orca adored, intriguing
Near death and extinction.
Money for the orca, killer whale and big black fish
Oh no! Money only for the orca
Not killer whale nor big black fish.

Hated or adored
Feared or intriguing
Feel for it how you will
Orca, killer whale or big black fish
Call it what you will
This big, beautiful creature will go, go
This big, beautiful creature is going, going
That big, beautiful creature is gone
Save our black fish
Sob.

Harriet Steele (12)
Rye St Antony School, Oxford

My Family And Other Animals

Granny Panda
Sleepy, lumbering, adorable, big, cuddly teddy bear
Queen of changing the subject
Crossword solver extraordinaire
Always on the wrong end of the bamboo stick

Mummy Hedgehog
Bonkers, a side-splitter, hilarious hairbrush
Sometimes prickly, super sensitive, trundling along
Crazy hair just like me, snout sniffing
Always creative and caring

Daddy Bumblebee
Humming, whistling, fuzzy and buzzing
Busy working, heavy, hovering and hoovering
A teaser, crowned king of awful jokes
Always clowning around

Brother Angry Bird
Humorous goof, a baseball cap beak
Infuriating curmudgeon, Olympic gold grump
Wonderfully witty, the brightest of bulbs
Always winding me up

I, Flamingo
All singing all dancing, acting bananas
Fantastic gymnastic, creepily flexible, double jointed
Proud to be pink, diva, achiever
Always the centre of attention.

Lucia Boué (12)
Rye St Antony School, Oxford

Tick

T he time orbits my head like an amaranthine torment
I ts pure pressure inching closer as the hours pass
C arelessly piling high
K ing of idleness

T he frustration etching into me
I ntolerable
C ontrolling me
K icking my spirits

T elling me how to spend my time
I rritated and bored
C ounting the minutes
K eeping me a prisoner

T error of sitting in silence
I gnorant of information
C ouldn't care less
K een to escape

T his is my homework
I ts papery dryness
C risp clear sound of scratching paper
K illing my time.

Sophie Lafferty (12)
Rye St Antony School, Oxford

The Squirrel In Manhattan

Amongst a school of giants
Lays a bed of green
Where the noise and the rushing is silenced
And nothing but beauty is seen.

For I am the core of the battlefield
The jungle revolves around me
And to see the concrete towering above
Casts a spell of mystery.

Each rectangle is a castle
Each turret houses them
Them being the invaders
Women, children and men.

A celebrity I am
In my own domain
As the invaders pass and try to tear
Through my barky, wooden frame.

As I stroll along my life path
My story forms its pattern
A small tail turns the legend
Of the squirrel in Manhattan.

Roisin Seacole (13)
Rye St Antony School, Oxford

A Winter's Evening

After a walk in the deep white snow
After a snowball fight with Gemma
After making snow angels with my dog
'Time to come in,' shouts Sophie.

Time to curl up on the sofa by the fire
Time for hot chocolate with fluffy marshmallows
Time for crunchy biscuits and juicy bones
Now is the time to relax.

Now the snow is softly falling
Now the fire is dying down
Now we both have heavy eyelids
Time to drift into dreams.

Madeleine Kaylor (12)
Rye St Antony School, Oxford

YOUNG WRITERS INFORMATION

We hope you have enjoyed reading this book - and that you will continue to enjoy it in the coming years.

If you like reading and writing poetry drop us a line, or give us a call, and we'll send you a free information pack.

Alternatively if you would like to order further copies of this book or any of our other titles, then please give us a call or log onto our website at www.youngwriters.co.uk

Young Writers Information
Remus House
Coltsfoot Drive
Peterborough
PE2 9BF
(01733) 890066